WHAT CHRISTIANS BELIEVE

AND WHY

'Christianity is a statement which, if false, is of no importance, and if true, of infinite importance. The one thing it cannot be is moderately important.'

C S Lewis

WHAT CHRISTIANS BELIEVE AND WHY

A Questioning Person's Guide

to

The Christian Faith

by

David Behrend

Grant Books, Worcestershire 2003

What Christians Believe, and Why
First published in the United Kingdom in 2003
by Grant Books

Copyright © David Behrend

All rights reserved

No part of this book may be reproduced or utilised in any form or by any means, electronic or mechanical, including photography, copying, recording or by any information storage and retrieval system, without permission in writing from the publisher

ISBN 0 907186 49 1

Typeset in 13 on 15 Perpetua
and printed in the UK by
Warwick Printing Co Ltd
Caswell Road, Leamington Spa CV31 1QD

Grant Books
The Coach House, Cutnall Green,
Droitwich Spa, Worcestershire WR9 0PQ
www.grantbooks.co.uk

Contents

Acknowledgements	*vii*
Preface	*ix*
Bible Quotations and References	*xii*

PART I: THE MAIN CHRISTIAN BELIEFS

The Starting Points

CHAPTER 1	*A Short Outline of What Christians Believe*	1
CHAPTER 2	*The Reasons for Believing in God*	5
CHAPTER 3	*The Bible, and how much of it is History*	13
CHAPTER 4	*Are Miracles Possible?*	30

Christian Beliefs about Jesus Christ

CHAPTER 5	*The Life and Death of Jesus Christ*	38
CHAPTER 6	*The Resurrection of Jesus Christ*	43
CHAPTER 7	*Some Events that Followed the Resurrection*	51
CHAPTER 8	*The Future Return of Jesus Christ*	58
CHAPTER 9	*The Virgin Birth of Jesus Christ, a Relatively Late Belief*	62
CHAPTER 10	*The Divinity of Jesus Christ*	68

God's Purpose and Plan in Creation

CHAPTER 11	*The Traditional Christian Beliefs about God's Purpose and Plan in Creation*	*78*
CHAPTER 12	*God must have a Purpose and Plan in Creation*	*84*
CHAPTER 13	*Life after Death*	*86*
CHAPTER 14	*Judgement, Heaven and Hell: the Consequences for the Next Life of how we Live in this Life*	*93*
CHAPTER 15	*What can we Understand of God's Plan in Creation?*	*98*
CHAPTER 16	*Why must there be so much Pain and Suffering in this Life?*	*109*
CHAPTER 17	*Why does God Hide his Presence from us?*	*129*

Part II: FOR THOSE WHO MAY WISH TO BECOME PRACTISING CHRISTIANS

CHAPTER 18	*Becoming a Practising Christian*	*135*
CHAPTER 19	*An Introduction to Prayer*	*146*
CHAPTER 20	*An Introduction to Reading the Bible*	*161*
CHAPTER 21	*Christian Belief about the Holy Spirit and his Place in Christian Life*	*169*

APPENDIX

The Apostles' and Nicene Creeds	*172*

Index — *174*

Acknowledgements

THERE will I am sure be those who wonder how an ordinary Christian, possessing no obvious qualifications to do so, could have come to write a book such as this.

A full answer to this question would require some pages of autobiography. The book was originally conceived, and the work for it started, a fair number of years ago, its conception being linked with my feeling that there was a need for a book that did not just assert and elaborate on Christian beliefs, but explained in a readily understandable way the main grounds for holding them.

The book that has finally emerged could certainly not have been written without the considerable help and encouragement of two people. One, in the early stages (he died in 1985) was my uncle, the Reverend Oswald Welsh, who was a Minister in the Church of Scotland, and for a number of years was Principal of St Paul's Theological College in Kenya. The other has been Canon Derek Fathers, who at the start was vicar of Thornton Hough. Derek in particular has given me an enormous amount of help, more or less from the beginning onwards. Apart from his guidance of my initial studies, he has read through successive drafts of the book, and made a large number of pertinent comments and suggestions for improvements. I am very greatly indebted to him.

I would also like to thank a number of other people who have kindly read and commented on one or more of the book's previous versions. I should first explain that besides typescript drafts there has been an earlier printed version: a small trial edition of the book was printed by W.H. Evans and Sons of Chester in March 2000. Copies of this were offered through advertisements placed in Thornton Hough Parish Magazine, and readers were invited to complete a questionnaire giving their reactions. Some thirty people very kindly did so, or commented in other ways, with several of them making more extensive suggestions for improving what I had written. The comments and suggestions I received have been of great help in my latest revisions of the book.

Before mentioning names I should stress that my doing so should not be taken to imply their concurrence, or near concurrence, with the views I express. Apart from Thornton Hough parishioners, I have deliberately sought comments from several people whose standpoints are different from my own: some of them have Christian beliefs that I know differ to some extent from mine, and others would count themselves as agnostics, if not atheists. This said, I would like to express my very sincere thanks to the Revd Ian Benson, Canon Dr Trevor Dennis, Mr Bob Grant, Mrs Caroline Lancelyn Green, Mr Chris Milne, the Revd John Peck, Mr Charles Povey, the Revd Derek Seber, Mr Maurice Temple Smith, Mrs Maureen Thompson and the late Mrs Ruby Turberville; also, and not least, to my late brother John and to my wife Ruth. All of them have made helpful comments or suggestions that led to changes in what I had previously written; several of them have made numerous detailed suggestions for improvements. Their combined contribution to the book has been a very large one.

I would like to record my thanks to a number of other people who read the trial edition of the book and returned questionnaires to me, whose names I will not mention, and who may not be aware that they have helped me. They have done so either through certain of their written comments, or through points they made in subsequent discussion group meetings about subjects covered by the book.

One other person to whom I owe a great deal of thanks is Audrey Ellison, who was my secretary before I retired from business, and has done most of the typing, latterly word processing, of the various drafts and redrafts of the book.

David Behrend
Thornton Hough, 2003

Preface

THIS book is about the principal Christian beliefs, and the reasons for holding them. The ground that it covers should be clear from the table of contents. I have written it for anyone, whether present Christians or not, who would like to enlarge their understanding of Christian beliefs and their rationale. It is meant especially for 'questioning' people – for those who may be inclined to question the truth of particular Christian beliefs, or who at any rate would like to understand how and why the Christian Church came to hold them.

According to the 2001 Census, over seventy per cent of the adult population of Britain identify themselves as Christians. To judge from the very much lower church attendance figures, that percentage must include a great many people who do not normally go to church services. I suspect that it also includes a good many who feel doubtful about some of the Christian Church's beliefs, and possibly also a fair number who do not have a very full understanding of what Christian beliefs actually are.

From the point of view of readers who may at present have only a limited knowledge of Christian beliefs, the book 'starts from the beginning', and assumes that you may know little or nothing about the Christian faith.

Among more knowledgeable Christians, as already indicated, the book is meant mainly for those who may feel doubtful about some of the traditional beliefs of the Church, and who are not altogether sure just what they should believe. This particularly applies to those who feel uncertain what to make of the Bible, and wonder how far it can be relied upon as being historically factual. Christians today have a range of different views about the Bible. There have always been different views about its interpretation. But this apart, until the second half of the nineteenth century it was generally regarded as so inspired by God as to be without errors of any kind: its authors wrote it entirely as God meant it to be. There are still many Christians who continue to uphold this traditional belief. But there are a great many others who do not think the Bible's authors can have been inspired in quite this way, or who are simply not sure about it, and it is these Christians who are most likely to find this book helpful.

If you yourself hold the traditional belief about the Bible, or something close to it, you may well find there are certain parts of the book, besides what it says about the Bible, with which you do not agree. But you could find it of interest for giving a fuller understanding of the viewpoint of Christians whose beliefs about the Bible differ from your own.

Different views on the Bible apart, there are a number of traditional beliefs of the Church that have come to be questioned among present-day Christians. Worldwide, the basic beliefs stated in the creeds of the Church probably remain accepted by the great majority of churchgoing Christians. But particularly among Christian theologians and scholars in the Western world, even if only by a minority of them, several of these beliefs are more or less rejected, or at least seen as open to serious doubt. A fair number of ordinary Christians may well have similar doubts.

In the course of the book, besides explaining the traditional beliefs of the Church, I will be mentioning the more important differences in belief that are held among Christians today. I also aim to leave readers in no doubt about my personal beliefs! So that you may know what to expect, I should say here that my beliefs about Jesus Christ are close to the traditional beliefs of the Church stated in the creeds. But on the subjects that are covered in the chapters about God's purpose and plan in creation (chapters 11 to 17), along with many other Christians today my beliefs on a number of subjects, such as 'judgement' and 'hell', differ from what was believed almost universally until the nineteenth century.

I do not expect that you, the reader, will necessarily be persuaded to share all my own beliefs. 'Questioning' people generally want to make up their own minds on what to believe, after making their own assessments of the evidence and arguments. The main purpose of this book is to put you in a position to do so.

You will, I hope, find answers that satisfy you on the most important questions of Christian belief. There are, however, two warnings I should give at the outset. The first is that, as questioning people today will generally see it, no individual Christian belief can be entirely *proved* to be true: it is always a matter of judging the probability of its truth. It is really only when you start to see how the different probabilities fit together into a coherent whole that they become more than probabilities, and close to certainties. The second warning is that you should not expect to find definite answers on all the questions the book will be discussing. Sometimes we have to be content with not really knowing the answer.

The first, and much the larger, part of the book is about Christian beliefs. There is also a second part, with four chapters, about starting to live as a practising Christian. This arrangement of the book, and the larger number of pages in the first part of it, may give the impression that I think what we believe is more important than how we live. I certainly do not think that! I do think, however, that generally speaking to become, and to continue to be, practising Christians, our lives need to be based on a reasonably firm foundation of Christian beliefs. That is why the book is as it is.

If you yourself would like to know from the start the answer to the question 'How do you become a practising Christian?' you can certainly read chapter 18 first of all. You do not need to have read all through Part I before you do so.

The Christian faith is about how God means us to live our lives. More fundamentally, it is about the real meaning and purpose of our present lives: why are we really here? To those who have no religious beliefs, this question may appear to have no sensible answer. We live in an all too disordered, cruel, confused and uncertain world – a world in which, for many people, it may now seem difficult to feel optimistic about the future. But Christians are able to be optimistic. We believe that beyond the turmoil, tribulations and injustices of our present world, life has a meaning and purpose. That meaning and purpose extend beyond this present life.

Unbelievers are apt to see Christians as people who have somehow been led, or misled, into believing what is really unbelievable. However, the Christian faith is far from being an irrational faith. Properly understood, its beliefs are not beliefs that have to be held more or less contrary to reason; but rather, they are based on a combination of historical evidence and reasoned argument.

Bible Quotations and References

WHERE particular passages in the Bible are either quoted or referred to in the text of the book, the references in brackets and italics give the title of the Bible's book, followed by the chapter and verse numbers. For example: *(Acts 1.9–11)*. The reference here is to the book entitled The Acts of the Apostles (which is often abbreviated to Acts) chapter 1, verses 9 to 11.

Quotations are sometimes from the New International Version of the Bible, sometimes from the Good News Bible. These are abbreviated respectively *NIV* and *GNB*.

Where Bible references rather than quotations are given, there is no need to look these up. They are given simply to indicate, for those who are interested, where relevant supporting Bible passages can be found.

PART I

THE MAIN CHRISTIAN BELIEFS

The Starting Points

Chapter 1

A Short Outline of What Christians Believe

THIS book is about why Christians believe as we do, and in the course of it each of the principal Christian beliefs will be considered separately. This chapter gives a brief account of all our main beliefs as they are normally understood. These beliefs fall under four headings: our beliefs about God, about Jesus Christ, about the Holy Spirit, and about God's purpose in creation. The latter heading embraces our beliefs about what happens when our present life is over.

Our beliefs about God
Our belief in the existence of God is the most fundamental of Christian beliefs. It is a belief that we share with Jews and Muslims.

Though the full nature of God lies altogether beyond our human comprehension, his main characteristics as Christians (and generally also Jews and Muslims) have come to understand them can be described as follows:

- He is a spiritual God, and thus hidden from us, not knowable to our normal human senses.
- He is the creator of the universe, the ultimate power within it, and the ultimate source of everything in it. However, although he is all powerful, he has chosen to accept the limitations of his power that flow from allowing human beings and other creatures to possess freedom of will, and from ordaining that the universe should be governed by what we call laws of nature.
- He is omnipresent – present everywhere.
- He is omniscient: he knows all that there is to be known; he is aware of everything that happens in our world and beyond.

- He is a loving God, and cares for every human person as a loving Father.
- He has an ultimate purpose in creation. It is a purpose that we can be sure is a good one, and human beings have a very important place in it.
- He is actively involved in our world, although in ways that are normally hidden from our view.

As is conventional, I have referred to God as 'he', and as a loving 'Father'. That should not be understood to mean that we believe God to be of male rather than female gender! God's being must be beyond gender. So far as we have to think of him in human terms, we can think of his 'fatherhood' as embracing also 'motherhood'.

There are a small number of people today who reckon themselves to be Christians, who do not believe in the reality of God, but consider that 'God' is, in effect, just a kind of idea within our minds. However, anyone who does not believe in the reality of God cannot really be a Christian, within the normal meaning of the name.

Our beliefs about Jesus Christ

It is our beliefs about Jesus Christ that primarily distinguish Christians from Jews and Muslims.

Jesus Christ lived his human life around two thousand years ago, in what are now Israel and Palestine. At about the age of thirty he became prominent among the Jewish people living there as a remarkable religious teacher, and also as a person who demonstrated extraordinary powers of healing.

Christians believe that Jesus Christ was much more than just an ordinary man. We believe that before his human birth he possessed, and continues to possess, the divine nature of God; that he was, and is, the Son of God. We believe too that he had no human father, but that his conception was a miraculous one, by the will of God.

After about three years of public ministry, occupied in both teaching and healing, Jesus was put to death by crucifixion. This was done at the instigation of the Jewish leaders, who had become greatly perturbed by various aspects of his teaching, and by the impact of his personality among the ordinary people, which they saw as a serious threat to their own authority. However – and this is really the central belief of the Christian faith – on the second day after his death Jesus was raised to life again by God. Following his miraculous resurrection he was seen on various occasions, over a period of several weeks, by a number of his closest followers.

Since that time, as indeed before his birth, he has been alive in spirit within the world, having the same nature as God.

It is our conviction that Jesus Christ came into the world to live his human life by the will of God, in order to show us the way that we are meant to live our own lives. He came also to show us the extent of God's love for us. Moreover, he opened the way for everyone who acknowledges him to escape from the chains of their past life, to start living the kind of life that God wishes us to live, in a growing relationship with him.

We have one other important belief about Jesus Christ. It is that some day in the future he will reappear within the world in some manifest and unmistakable way. This day of his reappearance will be one of great moment in the working out of God's purpose in creation.

Our beliefs about the Holy Spirit

Christians believe in the active existence of the Holy Spirit. The Holy Spirit can perhaps most simply be thought of as the spirit of God, actively at work within our world in certain ways.

Our beliefs about God's purpose in creation

Christians believe that God has a purpose in creation, which extends beyond the life on earth that we know. We believe that every person has a soul, which is our spirit, our true self, all that makes up our essential being, and that our souls will survive the death of our present physical bodies. This present life on earth – a life in which all that is good is so often overshadowed by the evils and afflictions of our world – is intended by God to be a kind of nursery for our infant souls. Our true destiny lies in the next life, though we cannot yet know what its real nature will be, beyond the curtain that we call death.

We believe also that after the end of this life we will all face some kind of 'judgement'. What happens to us in the next life will depend on how we have lived in this life. To be fit for the next life and enjoy it, we need to live now as God wishes us to live, and to become as far as we can the kind of people he wishes us to become.

* * * * *

A note on the Christian creeds
For many centuries the main Christian beliefs have been summarised in formal statements, called creeds. (The word 'creed' comes from the Latin word *credo*, meaning 'I believe'.) There are two such creeds in regular use today, known as the Apostles' Creed and the Nicene Creed, both being of ancient origins. The Nicene Creed is rather longer and more comprehensive than the Apostles' Creed, particularly in its statements about Jesus Christ.

I will be quoting a number of statements from these creeds, in modern English versions, as we come to look more closely at individual Christian beliefs in the chapters that follow.

The two creeds are set out in full in an appendix at the end of the book.

Chapter 2

The Reasons for Believing in God

I believe in God, the Father almighty, creator of heaven and earth. (Apostles' Creed)

As Christians see it, there are a number of different reasons for being convinced that God really does exist, and is not just, as atheists believe, a creation of human imagination. The main reasons could be said to fall under four different headings:

- the existence of our physical universe;
- God's actions in the birth, life, death and resurrection of Jesus Christ;
- evidence of God's actions in the continuing affairs of our world, including the evidence of miracles;
- evidence that God has on occasions revealed himself in an unmistakable way to individual men and women.

Various events that come under the middle two headings will be considered in chapters that follow. In this one we will concentrate entirely on the first and last of them.

Our physical universe as evidence of God's existence

Christians have always believed that our physical universe is the deliberate creation of God. We also see the existence of our universe, and of our world with all its many different forms of life, together with the many manifestations of order and design in everything that exists, as themselves providing convincing evidence of God's existence. Our universe and world, and life within our world, could not and would not have come into existence without God as their creator.

Until around the middle of the nineteenth century, when Darwinian theories about the progressive evolution of life on earth started to become increasingly accepted, it was generally believed that our universe and world were only a few thousand years old. The opening chapter of the Bible gives an account of their creation by God, in the course of six days, with the creation of the first man and woman, Adam and Eve, as the culminating event, and this account was widely believed to be essentially factual.

Scientists today, of course, give a very different picture of the origins of our universe and world, and of life within our world, which agrees with the Bible's imaginative account only in one important respect: they have not always existed. Our whole universe is now thought to have begun its existence around fifteen thousand million years ago, with some kind of enormous cosmological explosion, which is commonly known as the 'big bang'. Just what happened after this, during the following aeons, is far from being fully known; but the main sequence of events, so far as the creation of human life in our world is concerned, seems reasonably clear. Within our expanding universe there was the eventual emergence of our own solar system and planet; in due course there came the emergence of simple forms of life on our planet; then the gradual development of increasingly complex forms of life. Eventually, through the processes of evolution, there developed the highest forms of animal life we now know, including – sometime within the last few million years – our earliest humanlike ancestors.

There are some Christians known as 'creationists' – they are probably no more than quite a small minority of Christians in Britain, but certainly more in America – who reject the views of modern scientists about the creation of our universe and the evolutionary development of life within our world, and who continue to uphold the Bible's account of creation as being essentially the factual truth. To most Christians today, however, creationist beliefs, which disregard or grossly distort the evidence and arguments of science, are simply not credible. Although there remains much that is not yet known to science, and many of the relative details of what has happened in the course of evolution may still be open to debate, there is no good reason to discount the main scientific beliefs about the distant beginnings of our universe, and the gradual development of different forms of life on our own earth, culminating in the eventual evolution of human beings.

Some scientists believe in God, others do not. For those who have no belief in God, everything that now exists in our universe, and in our own world, is the result of an essentially fortuitous sequence of events that followed the big bang. The big bang itself was an apparently fortuitous event, which cannot at present be explained. What we know as the laws of nature, according to which our physical universe operates; our solar system and our world within it; the many different forms of life that have come into existence within our world; our own human existence: all are essentially accidental. They are just the way things have happened to turn out, in accordance with the way the laws of nature happened to establish themselves at the time of, or immediately following, the big bang. Though we do not yet have a full understanding of it, everything that has happened – from the big bang itself onwards – must in principle be fully explainable in scientific terms. There is no reason to think that an unknown supernatural mind and power, such as we call God, lies behind it all.

Christians, or at least most Christians, other than creationists, take a different view in one main essential. We can accept the scientific account of the way that things have happened since the big bang as being the truth, or something like the truth, so far as can be known at present. But we do not believe that everything that has happened – the coming into existence of our universe, and of our own world, and of the many different forms of life in our world, and of us ourselves – is simply fortuitous. We do not believe that the big bang with which everything started could itself have been an accidental event. (Apart from anything else, if, as some scientists reckon, the big bang involved some kind of enormous nuclear explosion, from where could have come the unimaginably immense source of compressed energy and power that must have been there before it could all start?) We believe that the whole of physical creation is the result of a deliberate act of creation by a supernatural Mind and Power, whom we call God. We believe that from the very beginning of creation, God intended and planned for events to follow more or less the course they have followed. We see the order and design of our universe and world, with all its incredible wonders and natural beauty, as the deliberate work of God. We see life itself, in all its many different forms, as the deliberate creation of God.

Christian beliefs about God as the creator and designer of the universe cannot be proved or demonstrated to be true beyond dispute. We believe that it must be so – or, as I think many Christians would say, we are totally convinced that it must be so. But in the end, given the present limitations of our human knowledge, that can only be a matter of personal judgement and perception.

No doubt the judgements we each of us make here will be influenced by whether or not we see other grounds, as well as the existence of our universe as it is, for believing in the existence of God. Christians of course do see other grounds as well as this for believing in God's existence. Atheists and agnostics do not see these other grounds; and, doubtless linked with this, they do not see the existence and design of our universe as compelling evidence for the existence of God. So if you personally are at present doubtful about God's existence, contemplating the wonders of our universe and world will probably not be enough in itself to remove the doubts you feel. You will need to consider also the other kinds of evidence for God's existence.

For those who accept that God is the creator and designer of our universe, there remains – inevitably – one ultimate mystery. It is the mystery that is summed up in the child's question, 'If God made the universe, who made God?' We may answer it, to the child, by saying simply that no one made God – he must just always have existed. But it is a mystery the answer to which must remain beyond our comprehension. We can only recognise that, in relation to everything that is, the full extent of our human knowledge and understanding does not yet amount to very much.

God's revelation of himself to individual men and women

For those who look, there is a fair amount of evidence that during the course of the past three or four thousand years, if not in earlier prehistoric times, God has on occasions revealed himself to individual men and women.

I am personally convinced that this is so. But because no one can be quite certain that someone else's claimed experience of God is 'real' and not imagined, it is not something that can be proved beyond any possible doubt. What is beyond doubt, however, is that there have been a number of people who have themselves become absolutely convinced that they have had real experiences of God. Evidence for this is to be found in various places within the literature of religion. What is also beyond doubt is that there are, and have been, a number of Christian theologians who, having studied the evidence more closely than most of us are able to do, have concluded that some people do indeed have real experiences of God.

But what is the nature of these experiences of God? And how can we reasonably judge whether someone else's claimed experience of God is real, not just an hallucination or a delusion, or even a pure fabrication?

To the first of these questions, what is it like to have an experience of God, there can be no simple answer. For, as seems clear from the evidence, the nature of these experiences can vary very greatly. God certainly does not appear to limit himself to a single method of revealing himself! However, I will not attempt to give an account of these different kinds of experience. Rather I will give two examples of just one such kind of experience – that in which there is a very vivid 'sense' of the presence of God.

In such an experience, it appears, the person has an overwhelming awareness of God's presence. There is an overpowering feeling of intense awe and 'holiness', and a vividly felt presence of another Being, an infinitely greater Being, who identifies himself quite unmistakably as God.

The two examples I will now give are the personally recorded experiences of James Hudson Taylor, and of John Wesley.

James Hudson Taylor (1832–1905) was one of the outstanding Christian missionary leaders of the nineteenth century. He was born and brought up in England, but spent much of his life in China. He was the principal founder of the China Inland Mission, which later became the Overseas Missionary Fellowship – an organisation still actively involved in Christian mission in a number of countries in East Asia. Greatly loved, admired and respected by those who knew him, he lived a life of remarkable devotion in the service of God and of his fellow men. He is here writing in his later years about the afternoon when as a young man, after much deep thought about how he could be of service to God, he went up to his room to pray, and to offer his life to him.

> Well do I remember as in unreserved consecration I put myself, my life, my friends, my all upon the altar, the deep solemnity that came over my soul with the assurance that my offering was accepted. The presence of God became unutterably real; stretching myself on the ground and lying there before Him with unspeakable awe and unspeakable joy, a deep consciousness that I was not my own took possession of me, which has never since been effaced.
>
> *(Quoted in Biography of James Hudson Taylor, by Dr and Mrs Howard Taylor – page 19, abridged edition, Hodder & Stoughton, 1973)*

John Wesley (1703–1791) was the leader of the eighteenth-century Christian revival movement in England, and he became the effective founder of the Methodist Church. A man of both prodigious physical stamina and notable intellect, who was a one-time fellow of Lincoln College, Oxford, he was also in every sense a great 'man of God'. He spent much of his long life travelling around the country, usually on horseback and in all weathers, to preach to many thousands of different audiences, large and small, quite often in the open air. Although his powerful personality sometimes led him to act rather autocratically, he was a man of great kindness and compassion, who frequently went out of his way to give help or comfort to people in need, difficulty or sickness. He kept a diary of his activities, which was later published as his Journal. It is in fact one of the classics of Christian literature, and still makes lively reading. In the following passage taken from it, he writes of the New Year night, 1st January 1739, when he and a number of fellow Christians met together for worship and prayer, at Fetter Lane Chapel in London.

> Monday, 1 January – Mr Hall, Kinchin, Ingham, Whitefield, Hutchins, and my brother Charles were present at our love feast in Fetter Lane, with about sixty of our brethren. About three in the morning, as we were continuing instant in prayer, the power of God came mightily upon us, insomuch that many cried out for exceeding joy, and many fell to the ground. As soon as we were recovered a little from that awe and amazement at the presence of his majesty we broke out with one voice, 'We praise thee, O God; we acknowledge thee to be the Lord.'

It is evident that in both the cases I have just quoted the writers themselves had no doubt whatever about the reality of God's presence.

And in the case of John Wesley, it would appear from what he wrote that his companions had no doubt either. But could they not have been mistaken?

When someone asserts that he or she has had an 'experience' of God, of the kind we are considering, there are broadly three main possible explanations of this claim. He may deliberately be trying to deceive us: he never had any experience of the kind he is claiming. Or he may have had some kind of hallucinatory experience, or have experienced some other kind of delusion of psychological or physiological origin. Though it seemed real to him, it did not stem from any reality outside his own mind; so in thinking he 'felt' God's presence, he was mistaken. Or his experience may in fact have been real: that is to say, God really was present and made his presence felt. A further possibility that may occur to some people is that the experience could stem from some form of spiritual reality other than God, misidentified as God.

There can be no absolutely certain way that we can tell, in any individual case, which of these explanations is the correct one. Of course, if you feel convinced yourself that God does not exist, or that if he does exist, he would never reveal himself to any human being in such a way, you will start by ruling out the third possibility. But if you have a reasonably open mind, then all you can do is to judge what looks to be the most probable explanation, using circumstantial evidence.

Thus we need to consider the person's life and known character, and to ask ourselves such questions as: can we seriously conceive of his being a deliberate liar? Or does his life lead us to believe that he is a man of integrity? Does our knowledge of him make it seem possible that he was deluded? Does he seem to be a person who is sometimes a bit out of touch with reality? And, more particularly, is he the kind of person who might not be able to judge the real nature of his experience? For like a vivid dream, an hallucination or a delusion may seem very real at the time; but one is normally able to make an intelligent judgement afterwards about its true nature. And again, how does his subsequent life appear to have been affected by his experience? Does his life bear witness to the probability that his call from God – if that was what he felt it to be – was a real one?

Within the Christian Church, where there is an acceptance that personal spiritual experiences may truly come from God, but do not always do so, there is a widely accepted test of their probable validity, or otherwise. It can be summed up as 'you will know them by their fruits'. That is to say, we can best judge according to the general evidence of the person's life. And by this test, we may reasonably conclude, both James Hudson Taylor and John Wesley were neither deluded nor deliberate liars: they almost certainly did experience the real presence of God.

In the Bible there are a fair number of references to occasions that appear to involve personal experiences of the divine presence. We will be looking at two such notable occasions later on, in chapter 7.

But, it may be asked, if it is true that God has on occasions revealed himself to certain men and women, why has he not revealed himself to everyone? Why should there be so relatively few people who have had these real experiences of God?

We cannot know the answers to these questions. Certainly, among Christians the most intense experiences of God's presence appear to be relatively exceptional. It could be that such experiences come mostly, if not only, to those who are receiving, or have received, some special call to his service.

Chapter 3

The Bible, and how much of it is History

IN the course of the book I will often be referring to what we can read in the Bible – the volume containing the Christian 'scriptures', ancient writings recognised as having a uniquely important status within the Christian Church. The Bible is our primary source on matters of Christian belief. The first section of this chapter gives a short account of what it comprises, and how it came to take its present form.

There are differences of view among Christians on a number of questions relating to the Bible. I will be commenting on some of these differences, in particular about the extent to which the Bible's authors were inspired by God to write as they did, and the extent to which the Bible records true history, in the second main section of the chapter. These questions apart, in the general description of the Bible that now follows, there are certain points on which other Christians would express views different from those that I give.

A short description of the Bible and its origins

The Bible is a collection of writings, known as 'books', by a considerable number of different authors, who wrote over a period of perhaps a thousand years, down to around the end of the first century AD. It is divided into two main parts, the Old Testament and the New Testament. Also included in some Bibles, but not in others, is a third part called the Apocrypha. The books it contains are of widely differing nature. However, the main theme running through the Bible as a whole is what in the eyes of its authors God has done: what he has done first of all in his relationship over a good many centuries with the Jewish people; and then what he has done through his Son Jesus Christ, who was born among the Jewish people. The central character of the Bible is God himself.

The Bible takes God's existence for granted. Its books were clearly written by authors who had no doubt about his existence, and for readers who did not doubt it either.

Christians quite often refer to the Bible as the word of God, a phrase that is usually taken to signify that God is in some way its ultimate author or inspirer, although there some different understandings about in what sense this is so. Certainly, whatever else the phrase may be seen to mean, within the Bible as a whole Christians find the expression of God's will and purposes for all people.

The Old Testament

The Old Testament forms the larger part of the Bible – about four-fifths of it, excluding the Apocrypha. The books it contains, which are of a varied nature, broadly formed the sacred scriptures of the Jewish people at the time of Jesus' life, and have continued to do so ever since. A number of them are substantially records of actual events in the history, and particularly the religious history, of the Israelite nation. Certain others, as many modern scholars think, may have little or no historical basis apart from their general setting, but are in the nature of imaginative stories with a religious message. (Commonly seen to be in this category are the books of Ruth, Esther, Job, Daniel and Jonah.) And some books could be partly historical, partly not: it is often not possible today to be sure how much of what we are told is factual history.

Another main group of books is those that contain the recorded teachings of the notable religious men who were known as prophets – men recognised by others as having been called by God to speak on his behalf. There are also some books that are a combination of religious and more secular philosophy; and there is a collection of religious poetry and prayers known as the Psalms. There is even a collection of love poems, called Song of Songs (sometimes also known as Song of Solomon, or Canticles).

The majority of English language Bibles contain a total of thirty-nine books in the Old Testament, but there are some that have forty-six. The difference arises because, from the sixteenth century onwards, there have been different views about whether seven relatively late books are sufficiently 'inspired' to be included in the Old Testament, as the Roman Catholic and Orthodox Churches hold, or are not so inspired and should be counted as part of the Apocrypha, as Protestant churches hold.†

Not much is known for certain about the authorship or precise origins of the Old Testament books. While some of them could be the work of single authors, or largely so, others are thought by many scholars to be compilations of different writings, which were put together into their present forms by unknown Jewish editors, from a variety of earlier written sources. In some cases, the earliest written records may have been preceded by periods of 'oral tradition', in which stories were passed on by word of mouth.

The dating of individual books as they now are is mostly also rather uncertain. However, the latest of them excluding the seven disputed books, usually reckoned to be Daniel, is thought to have been written about 165 BC.

The New Testament

The New Testament is all of more recent origin than the Old Testament, and is not much more than a quarter of its length. Centred on the life of Jesus Christ, it contains twenty-seven books, which fall into four main categories: the Gospels, of which there are four; the Acts of the Apostles, a single book; the Epistles, of which there are twenty-one, a number of them very short; and Revelation, a single book. Most of them were written between about 50 and 100 AD, that is, between around twenty and seventy years after the death and resurrection of Jesus; and it is generally agreed that they were all first written in Greek, which was the language most widely used in Asia Minor at that time.

The Gospels. For Christians the Gospels form the heart of the Bible. They are the accounts of the life, death and resurrection of Jesus Christ, and the records of his teaching, compiled by four different authors, known as Matthew, Mark, Luke and John. They are the main source of nearly everything we know about Jesus.

---

† The Protestant churches are those that were formed by Christians who broke away from the Roman Catholic Church in the Reformation of the sixteenth century, in 'protest' against some of its then practices, together with other more recently founded churches. The term originated from a formal protest (a 'Protestatio', as it was called) made in Germany in 1529, against an intolerant law passed by the Catholic authorities, which outlawed religious dissent.

Though there are certain differences of view on the subject, it is generally reckoned by the majority of New Testament scholars that the Gospels were all written between about 65 and 90 or 95 AD, with Mark's as the earliest and John's as the latest.

Matthew's, Mark's and Luke's Gospels all contain quite a lot of common subject matter, both narratives of events and accounts of Jesus' teaching, often with closely similar wording, although also with differences of detail between them. These three are known as the 'synoptic' Gospels, because of their similarities of content. John's Gospel, on the other hand, has a good deal of material, both narratives and accounts of Jesus' teaching, not found in any of the other three Gospels.

The Acts of the Apostles. 'Apostle' was the title given in the early Church to the twelve chief disciples of Jesus, and to one or two other leaders of the early Church. This single book tells the story of some main events in the first thirty years or so of the Christian Church, from the days immediately following the resurrection of Jesus in about 30 AD. Its author was almost certainly Luke, who also wrote the Gospel bearing his name, and who was evidently himself a participant in some of the later events he describes. It is commonly thought to have been written between 80 and 90 AD.

The Epistles. The Epistles are a collection of letters written, or dictated, by a number of leading figures in the early Church. The earliest of them, as most scholars agree, were written around 50 AD or very shortly afterwards, and are thus the oldest of the New Testament books. For the most part, it is clear that they were originally intended for reading within the particular Christian communities to which they were addressed, in various parts of Asia Minor, in Greece and in Rome. But there are some that appear to be more in the nature of tracts intended for fairly wide circulation; there are also four that were addressed to individual men.

The subject matter of the Epistles is quite varied. It includes instructions and advice on problems that had arisen within the communities to which they were addressed, together with encouragement to those who were facing persecution; also a fair amount of general guidance on the Christian way of life, and some discourses on matters of Christian theology. A number of them contain a certain amount of biographical detail and references to events, which serve to supplement The Acts of the Apostles as a source of information on the history of the early Church.

Revelation. This last book of the Bible is an 'apocalyptic' one. As that word signifies, it largely describes the writer's prophetic visions about the coming end of the world, about the final defeat of the powers of evil, and about the glories of life in the heavenly world that is to come. Much of it is written in a vivid, symbolic and poetic language, not very comprehensible to present-day readers. Its author is stated to be John; but it is not certain who he was. (Besides Revelation and John's Gospel there are three Epistles also ascribed to John. The question of who wrote each of them is discussed in the footnote on page 24 below.) It is commonly reckoned that the book was written about the mid-90s AD, with the main object of giving encouragement to Christians who were then suffering violent persecution under the Roman Emperor Domitian. At that time Christians were being put to death for refusing to acknowledge the Emperor as God.

The Apocrypha

The Apocrypha is a collection of Jewish religious writings which are of later date than most if not all of the Old Testament books, but earlier than those of the New Testament. When printed in Protestant Bibles the collection includes the seven books regarded as part of the Old Testament by Roman Catholic and Orthodox Churches.

The seven books of disputed status were originally included in an ancient Greek translation of the Jewish 'scriptures' (that is, books reckoned to be divinely inspired), which was known as the Septuagint, and was in use during the lifetime of Jesus. They were not included in Hebrew language Bibles, however; and around the end of the first century AD, because of doubts about their divine inspiration, they came to be excluded from all versions of the Jewish scriptures. They nonetheless continued to be accepted within the Christian Church as part of the Old Testament. However, at the time of the Reformation in the sixteenth century, in line with the now longstanding Jewish view, the breakaway Protestant churches rejected their scriptural status. As a result, they were removed from Bibles used by these churches. Following that tradition they are excluded from the majority of English language Bibles today.

The Apocryphal books are valued by Christian theologians as a source of information on the development of religious ideas during the last century or two before the birth of Jesus.

How and when the Bible was brought together

Though the individual books that make up our Bible were nearly all written before the end of the first century, it was not until towards the end of the fourth century that agreement was reached on just which books should be accepted as belonging to it.

As far as the Old Testament is concerned, it is clear that from the earliest days of the Church the Jewish scriptures (in their Greek Septuagint version) were accepted by Christians as being their own. This acceptance was a natural consequence of the fact that the first Christians, like Jesus himself, were Jews by birth and upbringing.

The creation of the New Testament, on the other hand, was a gradual process. What appears to have happened was that those early Christian writings that were found to be of most value were copied and recopied, to be circulated more and more widely among the different communities. Then, after a time, collections of different writings were brought together; and in due course, probably by around the end of the second century if not earlier, the main core of our present New Testament books had come to be widely accepted as having the status of scripture, on a par with the books of the Old Testament. For some considerable time after that, however, there were still certain books, Revelation being among them, the status of which continued to be a matter of some disagreement. As already indicated, it was not until later in the fourth century that all the remaining differences of opinion within the Church were finally resolved.

How closely do our present-day New Testament texts correspond with what was originally written?
Our modern English versions of the New Testament have been translated from Greek texts, which have themselves been derived from the earliest surviving manuscript copies. No original manuscript of any of the books has survived, nor have any first-century copies. The most important more or less complete New Testament manuscripts date from the fourth century, but there are a number of fragments and copies of individual books from the second and third centuries.

The earliest surviving manuscripts reveal a considerable number of variant readings, although the great majority of them are variants of minor significance. From the variations that are found, it is clear that textual alterations have occurred, whether accidentally or deliberately, in the course of the copying and recopying of early manuscripts. However, the substantial agreement in the main bulk of the surviving early manuscripts means that we can nonetheless be confident that our currently compiled Greek texts are most unlikely to be very much different from what was first written.

The historical reliability of the Bible

There are different views among Christians today on the question of how reliable the Bible is as a record of historical events.

Until about the second half of the nineteenth century, the Bible was generally thought within the Christian Church to consist of writings that were divinely inspired in such a way as to be infallible, without errors of any kind. There are still a good many Christians who hold to this traditional view (the 'conservative' or 'fundamentalist' view, as it is often called), and who believe in effect that the authors of the Bible were guided by God, or as is commonly said by the Holy Spirit, to write precisely as he intended them to write. In accordance with this belief, broadly speaking everything in the Bible that is written in the form of factual history must be altogether true history.

Among the many Christian theologians and scholars today who do not accept the traditional 'conservative' view of the Bible, the nature of its inspiration is seen differently, and there is a range of views on the question of how much of it is factual history. As regards its inspiration, most if not all non-conservatives would agree that the Bible's authors, and especially the New Testament authors, wrote in some way under the inspiration of the Holy Spirit. The exceptional spiritual quality of their writing bears witness to their inspiration. But whatever was the true nature of their inspiration (that really lies beyond our knowledge), it was not such as to make them infallible.

On the question of the Bible's historicity, any account of the different views that are held besides the traditional one needs to distinguish between the Old and New Testaments, as different considerations apply to each. Since our interest in this book is centred on Christian beliefs about Jesus Christ, and on the Bible's record of his life, and of the events that came soon after it, I will limit my comments here to the 'historical' books of the New Testament – the four Gospels and Acts. On these books, with some simplification, apart from the traditional conservative view there are two main different viewpoints, or schools of thinking, which can be labelled as 'conservative liberal' and 'radical liberal'.

Broadly speaking, in the conservative liberal view, the Gospels and Acts for the most part are substantially reliable as regards the principal events they describe. However the accounts of individual incidents may be inaccurate in detail, and a certain number of events depicted may possibly have little or no historical basis. Nonetheless, most of what we are told can be accepted as historically true, at least in its main substance.

In the radical liberal view, the Gospels and Acts have a much more limited historical reliability. A fair amount of what we are told is likely to be more or less fictional; this particularly applies to the records of apparently miraculous or otherwise out-of-the-ordinary events. However, stories that are not factually true can nonetheless convey profound truths. Many of the best writers through the ages have used fictional stories or dramas to express truths about human nature or about the characteristics of human societies. In a similar way, stories told in the Gospels and Acts can be seen as expressing religious truths, and especially what their authors saw to be truth about Jesus Christ. Such stories should be understood, and valued, as being 'symbolically' true, rather than factually true.

My own view is the one I have described as conservative liberal. Along with many other Christians, I see it as much more strongly supported by evidence and argument than either of the two alternative viewpoints.

The traditional conservative view that the authors of the biblical books were inspired by God in such a way as to make them incapable of error in everything they wrote is certainly one that many Christians today find it impossible to accept. Among the reasons for this, there is compelling evidence within the Bible itself – notably in the form of discrepancies between different accounts of the same events – that its authors were not immune from inaccuracies and mistakes of detail.

On the other hand, though the radical liberal viewpoint is difficult to refute altogether, there are no very persuasive arguments to support it; whereas there are solid reasons for holding a conservative liberal view. Radical liberals generally make one or both of two presumptions, each of which is very much open to question. One is that the authors of the Gospels and Acts were not particularly interested, or primarily interested, in recording factual truths: for them, 'religious truths' as they saw them will have been equally or more important. The other is that so far as they may have wished to record historical facts, they will have lacked reliable sources of information, and will have freely recorded stories that were derived from human imagination, whether their own or someone else's previously.

To put it more positively, there are good reasons for believing, first, that at least in the main the authors did seek to record historical facts; and second, that they will have had reasonably reliable sources of information available to them. To support these views, it is necessary to consider the two issues more fully; and it will be convenient to take the question of sources first. The extent to which imagination may have been used as a source will be discussed under the second heading of authors' intentions. Although parts of what follows will be relevant to Acts, we will concentrate primarily on the Gospels.

What sources did the Gospel authors use?
How far have New Testament scholars been able to identify the sources that the Gospel authors have used? To what extent are these sources likely to have provided reliable factual information? To answer these questions we need to work backwards from the Gospels as we have them.

There are many similarities between Matthew's, Mark's and Luke's Gospels. There are closely similar accounts of the same events, told in the same sequence; and there are, likewise, some very similar accounts of Jesus' teaching, especially in Matthew and Luke. It is now widely agreed among New Testament scholars that there are two main reasons for these similarities. One is that Matthew and Luke, who are generally thought to have composed their Gospels around 80–85, and it is not known which came first, both made extensive use of Mark's earlier Gospel, which was probably written around 65–70, as one of their principal sources. They did this particularly for their narratives of events in Jesus' ministry. The second is that Matthew and Luke, whose Gospels contain much more of Jesus' teaching than does Mark's, both almost certainly made use of an earlier written collection of Jesus' sayings, which has not itself survived as a separate document, for their records of this. The now lost record of Jesus' teaching is commonly referred to by scholars as Q (which stands for the German *quelle*, meaning source).

What is known about the original sources used for Mark's Gospel, and for Q? We will take Mark's Gospel first.

In general agreement, the author of Mark's Gospel was John Mark, whose name is mentioned in other New Testament books *(e.g. Acts 12.25; Colossians 4.10; Peter 5.13)*. Mark, as we are told by other early Christian writers, became a later life companion of Jesus' leading disciple Peter, and based his Gospel on what he learnt from Peter. It is fair to add, however, that a number of modern scholars, who form their views from close studies of the Gospel style and content, question the extent to which this was really so: they think quite a lot of it has the appearance of being based on oral tradition (memories that have been preserved by being repeatedly passed on by word of mouth) rather than on the first-hand memories of Peter. Parts of it also could be based on earlier written accounts drawn from oral tradition.

Whether Mark's Gospel was drawn primarily from the first-hand memories of Peter, or primarily from oral tradition, it is likely that in the main what we are told will be factual in its central substance. First-hand memories may themselves have been repeatedly retold, and simplified in the course of doing so, with possibly some alteration of detail, but the main substance would certainly be preserved. With oral tradition, although there might be more alteration of detail, much the same would otherwise apply: stories could become compressed with little or no detail, or some of the detail could get altered in the retelling, but again the central substance would be preserved. It should also be borne in mind that, particularly in the case of this relatively early Gospel, stories derived from oral tradition are unlikely to be more than second or third hand. Up to the time the Gospel was written, the main tellers of stories about Jesus will probably have been local church leaders no more than one or two 'generations' down from the original first-hand witnesses.

Turning now to Q, the record of Jesus' teaching, it is generally agreed that this must have been composed some years before Mark's Gospel. This is first because a written record of Jesus' teaching is likely to have been wanted within the young Church at a relatively early stage; and second because, if such a record had not already existed, Mark's Gospel would probably have contained much more of Jesus' teaching than it does. There are good reasons also for believing that it will have been compiled by a first-hand witness. There is an inherent likelihood that someone who was known to be a reliable witness will have been chosen to undertake this important task. And there is evidence that points to its having been done by Matthew, one of Jesus' closest followers, previously a tax collector, who was traditionally thought, though not generally by scholars today, to have been the author of the full Gospel bearing his name. The leading historian of the early Church, Eusebius (c.260–340), quotes a brief passage from an early second-century Christian writer called Papias: 'Matthew compiled the oracles in the Hebrew language. . .' If, as seems likely in the context, 'the oracles' refers to a collection of Jesus' sayings, then this will almost certainly be the collection modern scholars have called Q.

(That Matthew wrote the full Gospel bearing his name is now thought to be very unlikely: no close follower of Jesus would have used Mark's Gospel as a main source, since Mark – from what we know of him – was not a first-hand witness. What is much more likely is that Matthew's name became attached to the Gospel because he was known to have been the original source of important parts of it. The author of the Gospel as we now have it is not known.)

There are thus good reasons for believing that Mark and Q, which have been used as the sources for the greater part of Matthew's and Luke's Gospels, are both likely to be at least reasonably reliable. This means that Mark's Gospel as a whole, and also Matthew's and Luke's so far as they are drawn from Mark and Q, are all likely to provide fairly reliable accounts both of events that took place and of Jesus' teaching – reliable that is, in their main substance, though not necessarily in every detail, or in every word of Jesus' teaching. (With regard to Jesus' teaching, he himself is likely to have spoken in Aramaic, the main spoken language of Palestine at the time of his life; the Q record, according to Papias, was in Hebrew, although this may have been an Aramaic form of it; the Gospels were written in Greek; and our English Bibles are translations of Greek texts. We are thus two or three removes in translation from the first written records of what Jesus actually said.)

Apart from Mark and Q, how much is known about the sources used for the other parts of Matthew's and Luke's Gospels, and for John's Gospel in its entirety? I should first say with regard to Luke's Gospel that its author, though questioned by some modern scholars, is usually identified with the Luke who is described as a doctor in Paul's Epistle to the Colossians, and whose name is also mentioned in two other Epistles *(Colossians 4.14; 2 Timothy 4.11; Philemon 24)*. In other words, he will almost certainly have been a well-known person within the early Church, in close touch with other leaders. Also on the subject of authorship, the author of John's Gospel is a much debated issue. Though traditionally ascribed to the apostle John who was one of Jesus' closest disciples, and thus an eyewitness, a fair number of modern scholars question this.†

No specific Gospel sources other than Mark and Q have been identified with reasonable certainty. The existence of other intermediate

---

† There are five New Testament books ascribed to John – the Gospels, three Epistles and Revelation. Traditionally all five were thought to have been written by the apostle John. However, a number of modern scholars doubt this. There are seen to be significant differences in thought and language between the Gospel and Epistles on the one hand, and Revelation on the other, which suggest there were different authors involved. Also, while it seems quite likely that a single author wrote the Gospel and three Epistles, the second and third Epistles claim to have been written by 'the elder', who appears to have been a different John from John the apostle. However, there is no clear consensus of scholarly view on these subjects, and the traditional belief that John the apostle was responsible for all five books still has a good many supporters.

written records has often been surmised, and it seems inherently probable that there will have been some such sources that were used, although there is insufficient evidence to say with confidence what they are likely to have been. However, whether or not the Gospel authors used other earlier written records, every 'fact' that is recorded in the Gospels will ultimately have been derived from preserved memories – either the first-hand memories of original witnesses, where these were available, or oral tradition (which might be second-, third- or possibly fourth-hand memories, but seem unlikely to have been more remote than this).

In conclusion, looking at the four Gospels together, it is reasonable to believe that assuming the authors wished to record the true facts about Jesus they will have had a number of fairly reliable sources available to them. It is reasonable to think also that they will have chosen to use the sources they judged to be the most reliable.

We are left with the question of to what extent it really was the authors' intention to record factual information about Jesus, rather than to use imaginative stories to portray what they saw to be 'religious truths' about him. Before we come to that subject, however, there are two other general points about the factuality of the Gospels that need to be made first.

The first point relates to the sequence of events. In all the Gospels the sequence in which particular events are described may differ from their actual sequence, which the authors may not have known. Collections of different incidents and of Jesus' sayings appear to have been arranged in an order designed to suit the chosen structure of each Gospel. Linked with this, it is likely that incidents and sayings are quite often given to us divorced from their original context.

The second point concerns differences in detail between different Gospel accounts. As we have seen, Matthew, Mark and Luke have quite a lot of common ground between them. John's Gospel also has a certain amount of overlap with the others. Thus descriptions of particular incidents or events are very often found in two Gospels, quite often in three, and on occasions in all four. Much the same applies, though to a lesser extent, with the accounts of Jesus' teaching.

In most cases where the same events are described (and there is usually no real doubt that it is the same event) there are some differences of detail. Similarly with Jesus' teaching: the wordings we are given in different Gospels often have some differences, if only small. Some of the differences could be explained by the authors having used different sources, in which the details were different. The other main possible explanation is that for one reason or another – perhaps to reflect nuances of their own presentation or theological viewpoint, or the perceived needs of the particular Christian communities for which their Gospels were first primarily written – the authors made their own adaptations of detail. A good many liberal scholars (relatively conservative as well as radical liberals) tend to think that the latter explanation applies in most cases. Whatever the precise reasons the authors may have had for making such changes, they could well have reckoned that the detail as they received it from their sources would not always itself be entirely accurate.

The Gospel authors' intentions

Was it the primary purpose of the Gospel authors to record historical facts, so far as they could ascertain them? Or were the facts of secondary importance to expressing what they saw to be the truth about Jesus quite largely by means of imaginative stories? Or did they perhaps think it right to supplement the available facts with stories that were 'symbolic' of the truth, but were not factual?

I should first say that a good many scholars and theologians who take a relatively conservative view of the three synoptic Gospels take a more radically liberal view of John's Gospel, the last of the four to be written. John's Gospel is widely seen to be more theological in its approach than the other three: it appears to be especially concerned with expressing the author's understanding of the real nature of Jesus (an understanding that the Christian Church has generally come to share). There certainly appear to be some substantial points of conflict between the narratives in the synoptic Gospels on the one hand, and in John's on the other. Much of Jesus' teaching is also very different in content and manner of expression from what we are given in the other Gospels.†

The comments that follow apply primarily to the three synoptic Gospels. In the general view of conservative liberals, records of the known historical facts about Jesus are what the Gospel authors primarily sought to provide. Records of the known true facts about Jesus are what the young Church in its earlier years will almost certainly have wanted. Any account that was known among the Church leaders to contain a fair amount that was fictional would probably have received their condemnation, and would not have come into general use within the Church.

In evident support of this view of the authors' intentions is the short preface to Luke's Gospel. It is addressed to someone called Theophilus, whose identity is not otherwise known.

> Many have undertaken to draw up an account of the things that have been fulfilled among us, just as they were handed down to us by those who from the first were eyewitnesses. . . Since I myself have carefully investigated everything from the beginning, it seemed good also to me to write an orderly account for you . . . so that you may know the certainty of the things you have been taught. *(Luke 1.1–4, NIV)*

Taken at its face value (although radical liberals scholars have questioned how far it is right to do so), Luke's opening words are effectively stating that his purpose is to give a factual account of events.

To say that the Gospel authors set out to record the known facts about Jesus is not to say that they were unbiased historians – if there ever could be an altogether unbiased historian: historians select the material they wish to present, and they generally present it to support certain conclusions they themselves draw. The Gospel authors were all convinced Christians: they were in no doubt themselves that Jesus Christ was the Son of God, and they intended to leave their readers in no doubt about this too. The Gospels are presented accordingly.

It is possible that sometimes the authors will not have known if certain of the stories that reached them had no factual origin; but it is

---

† The most significant conflict, or apparent conflict, between the narratives of the synoptic Gospels and John's Gospel relates to Jesus' Messiahship. In the synoptic Gospels Jesus is portrayed throughout his ministry as being very reticent to make any public claim that he is the Messiah. *(See especially Matthew 16.20, Mark 8.30.)* But in John's Gospel he is portrayed as acknowledging his Messiahship from the outset of his ministry. *(See John 1.49–51 and 4.25–26.)* Quite a lot of the teaching of Jesus given in John's Gospel, in which he makes assertions about himself and his relationship to God, also appears to be inconsistent with the reticence of the synoptic Gospels.

unlikely that they will mistakenly have included a substantial number of fictional stories. Going back to the earliest days of the Church – which, as we will see later, was effectively founded very shortly after the death and resurrection of Jesus – the stories that first came to be told and retold about him will almost certainly have been factual. If later on some of the stories became heavily embroidered or distorted by certain of those who told them, or if some entirely imaginative stories started to be told, they are likely to have been widely recognised as such – in the earlier years among those who had known Jesus personally, and later among the established Church leaders. That would not necessarily have prevented their continuing repetition; but it seems unlikely that many such stories would have become part of the accepted tradition about Jesus, to be recorded in the Gospels.

Many conservative liberals would allow that, perhaps especially where factual information was lacking, the Gospel authors may on occasions have used their own imagination in their accounts of certain incidents or events. But this will not have happened very much.

Radical liberals take a different view from the one I have just given. In their judgement a good many embroidered or entirely imaginative stories about Jesus will have become told, and widely repeated, over the years before the Gospels were written. The Gospel authors will either have accepted them as the truth, and retold them as such in their accounts; or, if they knew or suspected that the stories were not factual, they will have included them for the symbolic truths they were seen to portray. In many cases, they may themselves have been the creators of the stories.

For the reasons I have given, along with conservative liberals generally, I think that radical liberal views along these lines are mistaken.

In practice, it is particularly on the accounts of miracles and other out-of-the-ordinary events that radical liberals take different views from those of conservative liberals about whether what we are told is likely to be substantially factual. Broadly speaking, conservative liberals, myself among them, are ready to believe that real miracles can happen, and that most (though not necessarily all) of the New Testament miracle stories could well be more or less factual. Radical liberals, on the other hand, tend to take the view, on general principles, that real miracles are unlikely to have happened. The stories of apparent miracles or other abnormal events can hardly be factual stories of real miracles or actual events. Thus, while the Gospel accounts of Jesus healing many people may well be true in their main substance — there can be no doubt that he healed many people — the healings cannot really have been miraculous. Other miracle stories should be seen not as factual, but as imaginative stories symbolic of the truth about Jesus' nature.

To what extent the views of radical liberal scholars and theologians about the likely nature of the New Testament stories of miracles and other extra-ordinary events are coloured, or determined, by prior convictions that real miracles are very unlikely is hard to judge. But anyone who believes that real miracles are very unlikely to have happened — and there are probably quite a lot of Christians today of whom this is true — is almost bound to be a radical liberal in their views about the historical reliability of the Gospels and Acts.

In the chapters covering Christian beliefs about Jesus Christ we will be looking at a number of the most important out-of-the-ordinary events described in the Gospels and Acts, starting with the resurrection, on which there are different views among Christians about what is likely to have happened. Before that, in the next chapter, we will consider the general question of whether there really can be miracles — events that could not normally happen, and can only be attributed, if they actually did happen more or less as described, to some deliberate act of God.

To conclude the present chapter there is a general point that needs to be made, or remade, about the Gospels. Much of the last few pages' description of the conservative liberal view of the Gospels to which I subscribe has drawn attention to reasons why they may not be altogether factual. This may possibly have given a somewhat negative view of their value. So I would like to end by stressing my personal conviction, which is certainly shared by a substantial proportion of Christian theologians and students of theology, that although the Gospels may not be factually accurate in every detail, they nonetheless give collectively an essentially true portrayal of the principal events of Jesus' life, and of his teaching. Equally important, they faithfully depict the kind of man that he was.

Chapter 4

Are Miracles Possible?

THIS chapter discusses the general question of miracles. A short separate section at the end of it comments on another kind of abnormal event that quite often occurs in the Bible, the appearance of angels.

The Bible contains a good many stories of miracles and other out-of-the-ordinary events. They are to be found both in a number of Old Testament books and in all five of the 'historical' books of the New Testament, the four Gospels and Acts. The events in question take a variety of forms. In the New Testament, apart from the miracles of Jesus' birth and resurrection, other miracles we are told about range from extra-ordinary healings, to dead people being raised to life, and miraculous feedings of large numbers of people. The healings, of which there are a good many different accounts, include blind people having their sight restored, lepers being instantly cured, severely crippled people becoming able to walk again, and people suffering from some gross psychological disturbance being restored immediately to sound mind. Besides miracles, there are also accounts of appearances of angels, and of voices from heaven.

The accounts we are given of these events are usually very brief, although there may sometimes be a fair amount of surrounding detail. But they are generally told in a way that makes it clear that the authors of the stories see them, and intend their readers to see them, as involving deliberate acts of God himself.

Can there really be miracles – that is, events that are contrary to the established laws of nature, or that could not otherwise normally happen, brought about by an exceptional act of God? Are the Bible stories of miracles to be accepted as more or less factual descriptions of extra-ordinary events that really did take place? Or should we share the views of radical liberal theologians and scholars, who generally believe that the miracle stories told in the Bible cannot be factual, but should be understood in some other way or ways?

More or less by definition, those who do not believe in God will not believe there can ever be such a thing as a miracle. But it is also true to say that, living as we do in a scientific age, in which we are accustomed to think of every physical event as having a rational explanation in terms of physics, chemistry or biology, a fair number of Christians have also come to doubt whether miracles have ever really happened. For they find it hard to believe that God could, or would, cause anything to take place that is contrary to the normal laws of nature. Even if he were able to do so, he would surely never interfere with the established natural mechanisms of his creation.

In line with what the Christian Church as a whole has believed from the beginning, probably the great majority of churchgoing Christians today do believe that real miracles can happen, and on occasions have happened. But are they right to believe so?

It first needs to be said that, sometimes at least, apparently miraculous events could have some natural explanation, which lies beyond our present understanding of what we call the laws of nature. Our knowledge of how nature works is growing all the time, but it is still far from complete, and there is much that we do not yet understand. Two hundred years ago, if anyone had heard the sound of a radio, that could have seemed to be a miracle, but we do not regard it as such today! So when nowadays, as can sometimes happen, we hear of a 'miraculous' case of someone being healed in an unusual way from an apparently incurable illness, was it really a miracle, or did it have some natural explanation beyond our present understanding?

It seems possible that at least some of the apparently miraculous healings performed by Jesus could have had some unknown natural explanation. But there are a number of miracle stories in the New Testament where this hardly seems to be conceivable. The miraculous conception of Jesus, and his resurrection, are two such cases, and there are others such as the accounts of people he raised from death. Either they actually did involve miracles – deliberate acts of God, outside the normal workings of nature – or the accounts we are given cannot be factual.

Assuming you believe in the existence of God, who has created the universe, and who in some sense must have ordained the laws of nature, and determined the ways in which our natural world will normally function, there appear to be three main possibilities so far as miracles are concerned. These are:

- God has created and ordered our physical universe in such a way that it is impossible for him ever to intervene in the course of natural events.
- Though it would be possible for God to intervene to override the normal laws of nature, in practice it is not something he would ever do.
- God has left himself with the possibility of intervening to override the normal laws of nature, and causing things to happen in ways that are different from normal; and on certain occasions, he has in fact done so.

If you think that the third of these possibilities is not to be dismissed, then you will think that miracles are at least a possibility – though of course you may still have reservations about whether any particular reported event really did involve a miracle. If on the other hand you think that the first or second of the possibilities is much more likely than the third, then you will naturally be inclined to rule out the possibility of miracles.

The latter is the position generally taken, whether consciously or subconsciously, by radical liberal Christian theologians who see the Bible accounts of miracles as being symbolically rather than factually true, or in the case of healing stories as having some kind of natural explanation.

I see no reason myself to rule out the third of the three possibilities listed. It does in fact seem to me to be inherently more likely than the other two possibilities. So I do believe there can be real miracles. And combining this with the view that in the main the Gospels and Acts are historically quite reliable, I think that the majority of miracle stories told in the New Testament are likely to be more or less true accounts of actual events. The majority, but not necessarily all: it could still be that in one way or another a certain number of imaginative stories, or imaginative developments of factual stories, have found their way into the Gospels and Acts.

With the Old Testament stories of miracles I think there is a greater degree of uncertainty than with the New Testament. Most of the Old Testament miracle stories are connected with three leading prophets of Israel – Moses, Elijah and Elisha – all relatively early figures, living from the thirteenth to the ninth centuries BC. The greater uncertainty is essentially because, while there are good reasons for believing that the Gospels and Acts are substantially historical in their records of the main events they describe, with the Old Testament there is generally more uncertainty about whether particular stories are historically based or not. In many cases we do not know enough about how the books came to be written, and about the sources their authors used, to make confident judgements. But that said, for those who believe in the possibility of miracles, there is no good reason to think that in Old Testament times there will not have been at least some such miracles as those that are described.

But, it may be asked, if God really can perform miracles, or can empower human beings to do so, why does he not do so more often? The answer, or part of the answer, could well be that the reasons that led him to create a physical universe governed by laws of nature will always require that miracles should remain very exceptional events. As it is, because they are so exceptional, for practical purposes we can continue to rely on the fact that we live in a natural world that behaves in a predictable way. If miracles were to become much more common than they have been, our natural world would cease to be reliably predictable.

We cannot know in what rare circumstances God will cause miracles to happen. But it appears that when they do occur, apart from their direct results, they may at least sometimes be intended to serve a wider revelatory purpose – that is, to be a means by which God reveals something of himself to mankind. Thus they can be proofs, for those with eyes to see, of his continued active involvement in our world. Certainly, the miracles performed by Jesus were seen within the early Christian Church as being among the proofs that he was no ordinary man.

To what extent there have been miracles in the course of subsequent centuries is not a subject we need pursue here. In chapter 7, however, I will be giving an account I happen to have seen of a fairly recent miracle.

Appearances of angels

Along with miracles, appearances of angels are another fairly common form of out-of-the-ordinary event described in the Bible, in both the Old and New Testaments. How are we to regard these accounts?

First of all, what are angels? As usually understood, angels are spiritual beings who are attendant on God in heaven. They also sometimes serve as messengers between God and human beings; and in this capacity, as it appears, they can temporarily take some bodily form. In the Epistle to the Hebrews, angels are described as 'spirits who serve God and are sent by him to help those who are to receive salvation' *(Hebrews 1.14, GNB)*.

Do angels really exist? It seems clear that the Bible authors had no doubts about the reality of angels' existence. Jesus Christ himself is recorded as referring to them a number of times, and the Christian Church as a whole has always accepted their existence. Probably a substantial majority of churchgoing Christians today continue to do so. But there are probably also a fair number who feel a bit uncertain, and some who are sceptical.

I see no reason myself to think that the Christian Church is likely to be mistaken in its belief about the existence of angels. That view has been reinforced recently by my reading a book that contains a collection of personal accounts of present-day encounters with angels.[†] The clearly abnormal incidents that are described are of a varied nature, some of them involving visual appearances, others not. It could perhaps be that some of those who have told of their experiences were mistaken in attributing them to the real appearance or action of angels; but I would certainly not want to dismiss all such attributions as bound to be mistaken. I do believe that there are almost certainly more living realities in our cosmos than are known within the normal experiences of human beings, and that some of these realities may occasionally impinge on our own lives.

I must confess, however, that I never feel altogether sure what to make of the accounts of angels' appearances in the Bible. Some of the stories could well be factual, or substantially so, while others may be imaginative. Another possibility that could sometimes apply is that the

---

[†] *Angels – True Stories of How they Touch our Lives*, by Hope Price; Macmillan, 1993; Pan Books, 1994.

account we are given has a factual basis, but should not be taken entirely literally. It may be the writer's method of telling us that, in some way that would be difficult to relate accurately, God was directly involved in what happened, and (it could also be) made his presence felt among those who were there. The person or persons present had some kind of God-given 'visionary' experience – an experience that certainly came from God, but which could not adequately be described in straightforward terms.

Some concluding comments

One of the penalties of taking a conservative liberal view of the Bible is that we are quite often left feeling uncertain about particular stories of miracles and other abnormal events. We cannot share the certainties of conservatives that they are always essentially factual accounts of real extra-ordinary events. Nor can we share the convictions of radical liberals (or at least, of the most radical of them) that such stories must be essentially fictional; or, that if they are partly factual, nothing out-of-the-ordinary could really have occurred. We occupy an in-between position, which may seem to be a rather unsatisfactory one.

Fortunately, however, when we come to look specifically at the most important events for Christian belief, it is not too difficult to make some fairly confident judgements about what is likely to have happened. In the course of the next few chapters on Christian beliefs about Jesus Christ, that is what I will be seeking to show. For each event we will be considering, our starting points will be, on the one hand, that we are not bound to take the Bible accounts we are given as being factual; but, on the other hand, that real miracles or other abnormal events do not have to be ruled out.

Christian Beliefs about
Jesus Christ

Chapter 5

The Life and Death of Jesus Christ

I believe in Jesus Christ, [God's] only Son, our Lord. He was conceived by the power of the Holy Spirit and born of the Virgin Mary. He suffered under Pontius Pilate, was crucified, died, and was buried. (Apostles' Creed)

CENTRAL to Christianity is the person of Jesus Christ. Christians believe that he has combined in himself the natures of both God and man, of both divinity and humanity.

In this chapter we will look at the principal features of his human life, as we can learn about it from the four Gospels. In the chapters immediately following we will go on to consider the main events that have led Christians to believe in his divinity.

There was a theory which at one time had some popularity in Britain, that Jesus Christ was a purely mythological figure who never actually existed. This view probably does not have very many serious adherents in the Western world today. However, it has been taught as an element of Marxism, and it may well still be widely believed in countries where communist philosophies have prevailed. It may also be that quite a lot of other people feel a little bit uncertain. To them, it will seem clear that the Bible contains a good deal that cannot really be historical; so what about Jesus himself?

There is no doubt whatsoever that Jesus Christ was a real person. While, as we have seen, there are some divergent views among scholars and theologians about how reliable are the four Gospels' accounts of Jesus' life, the books of the New Testament collectively provide overwhelming evidence of his having lived and died during the first thirty years or so of the first century AD.

The Life and Death of Jesus Christ

Outside the Bible there is a variety of further early written evidence of Jesus' existence. It is to be found both in a number of early Christian writings that do not form part of the Bible, and in a small number of references to Jesus in Roman and Jewish literature of the first and second centuries. While none of these authors were themselves eyewitnesses to the life of Jesus, their comments help to place him, and the early Christian communities, in the context of other historical events in the world at large. To Roman historians, the events of Jesus' life in the outlying province of Judea could hardly have seemed very important; so we could not expect that he would be regarded by them as a significant figure.

Jesus was born in Bethlehem in Judea, which was then a Jewish kingdom within the Roman Empire. As we are told, his parents had gone there from their home village of Nazareth in the district of Galilee, to take part in a Roman census; and because there was no room for them in the local inn, Jesus was born in a stable. Though the year of his birth is uncertain, this is generally reckoned to have been no later than 4 BC, and possibly up to three or four years earlier. (He was born during the reign of the Jewish King Herod, who is known to have died in 4 BC.)

Jesus' mother was called Mary; and she married Joseph, who was a carpenter. However, as Matthew's and Luke's Gospels both record, Joseph was not the true father of Jesus; for Mary's conception was a miraculous one, through the power of the Holy Spirit.

Beyond the events surrounding his birth, not much is known about Jesus' early life, apart from a single story of a visit to the Temple in Jerusalem when he was a boy of twelve, narrated by Luke. However we are told that he continued to live with his parents in Nazareth, and that he worked as a carpenter. For the rest, Luke writes simply that he 'grew in wisdom and stature, and in favour with God and men' *(Luke 2.52, NIV)*.

Shortly before Jesus himself became a prominent figure, there appeared a man known as John the Baptist (who as Luke tells us was a relative of Jesus), who became widely recognised as a prophet – one called by God to speak out publicly on his behalf. John preached by the banks of the river Jordan, where many came to hear him. In the name of God, he called people to repentance, to change their whole manner of life; and he baptised in the Jordan those who responded to his message and confessed their sins. He also proclaimed that after him would come one who was greater than himself, whose sandals he was not worthy to unfasten.

Just before the start of his own public ministry, Jesus himself came to be baptised by John. Immediately after his baptism, as all four Gospels relate, he received his commission and blessing from God, through the coming upon him of the Holy Spirit, for the work he was about to commence.

Sometime after this, John's public preaching was brought to an end by his arrest and subsequent death on the orders of Herod (a son of the Herod in whose reign Jesus was born), the vassal King of Galilee. For he had taken exception to John's criticisms of his unlawful marriage to his brother's wife.

Jesus' unique ministry of teaching and healing started when he was about thirty years of age; and it continued until his death, probably around three years later. Travelling around the countryside and villages, mostly with the twelve men he had chosen as his closest disciples, who later came to be known as the apostles, he taught about the kind of life that God meant people to live. The extraordinary authority of his teaching, which in form and manner was unlike anything those who listened to him would ever have heard before, often attracted large crowds.

Apart from his teaching, Jesus also spent much of his time healing those who were suffering from serious illnesses, physical disabilities or mental disorders. Quite often these cures appeared to be miraculous: people who were to all appearances incurable were nonetheless restored to health. On three occasions, we are told, he even brought back to life people who had died.

What kind of man was Jesus? Any attempt to describe his nature must be inadequate; but when we read the four Gospels we can find that he is brought to life by their portrayal of his words and actions, so that we are able to see some of the principal facets of his character. Thus we can see his great concern for others, and his limitless compassion for those who were suffering. We can see his unsurpassed wisdom, his deep understanding of human nature. We can see his quiet but compelling authority, his mastery of every situation. We can see his patience in adversity. We can see his total lack of arrogance or conceit. And above all, we can see his unique sense of closeness to God, his total devotion to him.

It was surely inevitable that Jesus should find himself in conflict with the Jewish religious authorities. Jewish religion at that time had come to place much emphasis on adherence to outward practices, such as customs of eating and fasting, and strict observance of the Sabbath day (Saturday), on which many forms of ordinary activity were forbidden. Jesus openly criticised the narrow legalistic way in which the religious laws were being interpreted and applied. He saw that an excessive emphasis on the details of religious rules, regulations and rituals all too often meant neglecting the things that really mattered, which lay at the heart of his own teaching, namely a person's real relationship with God, and the practice of true justice and of genuine care for others.

The growing antagonism and resentment of the Jewish leaders towards Jesus may well have begun with his challenging attitudes to some of the current religious practices. But besides this, they clearly saw his increasing popularity and following among the ordinary people as undermining their own influence and authority. There were some who were saying that he was the promised Messiah – the long-awaited religious and political leader, whose coming had been foretold by the prophets of old, who was expected to lead the people of Israel into a new age of greatness and glory. There was no saying where things might end, if he was allowed to continue at large. There were growing risks of disturbances to the peace. There was also a real danger that the Roman authorities would then be driven to some more active intervention in Jewish affairs.

In the minds of the Jewish leadership, Jesus came to be regarded as a serious menace to the stability of the established order, someone who had to be removed from the scene – and preferably in a way that would show him up as being the impostor he must surely be.

So it was that Jesus came to be arrested, like most political arrests at night (after betrayal by one of his disciples, Judas Iscariot), during his visit to Jerusalem on the occasion of the annual Passover festival – the most important celebration in the Jewish religious year. So it was too that the Jewish leaders managed to procure his sentence to death by crucifixion – a sentence they had to induce the Roman governor Pontius Pilate to pronounce, since they themselves had no powers to inflict capital punishment.

As the Gospels make clear, Jesus had foreseen how his ministry would end: he warned his disciples about it several times in the course of the final weeks, although they evidently found it hard to believe that it would be so. Though we are not told, he almost certainly will have realised from the very beginning that he was bound to find himself in growing confrontation with the Jewish authorities; and he will surely also have realised to what this would ultimately lead. But as he must have seen too, the only way he could have avoided the terrible end he had to face would have been to abandon his ministry.

For the sake of all that he had come to do, he was willing to die in the way that he had to die.

The death that Jesus had to suffer, after a severe flogging and a number of other preliminary brutalities had been inflicted upon him, was a common one – for criminals, slaves and suchlike – in those times. It was not only a particularly cruel and horrible form of death, but it was also regarded as a mark of ignominy, appropriate for those who were of altogether disreputable character. Thus the fact that Jesus was put to death in this way would surely discredit his name, completely and beyond repair: so the authorities must certainly have hoped and intended.

Chapter 6

The Resurrection of Jesus Christ

On the third day he rose again. (Apostles' Creed)

ON the second day after his death – on the 'third day', according to the then method of reckoning – Jesus was brought back to life again by God.

What are the grounds for this remarkable assertion, the assertion on which the Christian faith is really founded?

The Gospels give differing accounts of the events surrounding Jesus' resurrection, but they are all agreed that two days after his death, early in the morning, certain of his closest followers went to the tomb in which his body had been laid, and found it was no longer there. Then, though we have more varied records of what happened next, during the course of the same day he was seen – alive! – by a number of his close followers; and while he was with them he actually spoke to them.

Over the next few weeks there were a number of other occasions on which he appeared among those who had been with him during his ministry. Finally, a month or so after his death, he appeared to his closest disciples for the last time. It was then made clear to them that this would be the last time they would see him and talk with him. Thereafter, they understood, he would be in heaven. But one day in the future, he would in some unmistakable way come back again.

To many readers, and certainly to those who are not already convinced Christians, the Bible stories about Jesus' resurrection have an air of unreality about them. How could such things really have happened: the stories must surely be in the nature of legends? Moreover, none of the Gospels really agree in their descriptions of the supposed events. Does not this itself indicate that the accounts are imaginative?

With little doubt, a good many ordinary Christians have felt uncertain about what to make of the Gospel accounts of Jesus' resurrection. Can we today tell whether these accounts are more or less factual (extra-ordinary facts, certainly), or are essentially fiction?

Whatever actually did happen, there are three historical facts it would be difficult to dispute seriously. The first fact is that, very shortly after the death of Jesus, a group of his closest followers came to be convinced that he had been raised from death by God. The second fact is that it was on the strength of this belief that this group of people started to proclaim the Christian gospel, the heart of which was this claim about Jesus' resurrection from death. The third fact is that among those who shared the belief in Jesus' resurrection were the authors of the various different books of the New Testament – the earliest of which, as we have seen, was written about twenty years after his death.

The main evidence for these facts is to be found in the books of the New Testament. The third – the various authors' own conviction about Jesus' resurrection – appears self-evident from the way that they write. The first two – the conviction of Jesus' disciples, and within a few weeks of his death their proclamation of the news of his resurrection – is what we are told by Luke in the opening chapters of The Acts of the Apostles. And though there can be room for reservations about whether Luke's record of events is in every respect factual, there is no good reason to doubt that he is correct in the main essentials of what he tells us. Indeed, everything that is now understood about the history of the early Church – gleaned from both the biblical records and other comparatively early Christian sources – points unequivocally to the same conclusion.

Thus it is as certain as can be that the belief in Jesus' resurrection was *the belief on which, very shortly after his death, the Church was effectively founded.* The belief was not one, as is sometimes rather ignorantly suggested, that emerged a number of years after the death of Jesus and the foundation of the Church (a view for which there is no supporting evidence or argument of any substance). It was those who from the beginning were convinced that Jesus Christ had been raised from death who formed the nucleus of what became the Christian Church. If it had not been for this conviction there would never have been a Christian Church.

What was it then that led this group of Jesus' followers to become convinced that he had been raised to life by God – so convinced that they started to proclaim what we now know as the Christian faith, on the basis of their belief?

According to the Bible stories, it was the finding of the empty tomb two days after his death, and then his various appearances to his followers during the next few weeks. The disappearance of his body from the tomb could hardly in itself have led to a belief in his resurrection, for there was always the possibility that someone could have removed the corpse. It could surely only have been some convincing, or apparently convincing, reports that a number of people had actually seen Jesus alive that could have led to the general belief in his resurrection.

But what could have been the real origin of these reports of Jesus having been seen alive? There appear to be three main possible kinds of explanation, namely:

- There could have been some form of conspiracy among a certain number of Jesus' followers to present a story that was in fact a complete fabrication.
- A number of Jesus' disciples may have had some kind of visionary experiences, as a result of which they genuinely believed they had seen and heard him; but their experiences were in the nature of hallucinations, with no basis in reality.
- The disciples actually did see and hear the 'real' Jesus alive (whether or not it was his 'same' earthly body that they saw).

Naturally, anyone who believes that God is very unlikely to have raised Jesus from death in the miraculous way that the Gospel accounts indicate – and even more, anyone who does not believe that God really exists – will dismiss the last alternative. But assuming that you have a more or less open mind, let us discuss each of these possibilities in turn.

A conspiracy
The theory of a deliberate conspiracy is surely implausible. Could we really imagine that a group among Jesus' disciples – shattered as they must have been by his death – could have conceived such an unlikely idea,

agreed on it among themselves, and somehow gained the confidence and assurance to convince their fellow disciples and others that it was true? And would these conspirators have continued to publicise their claims against the strong opposition of the Jewish authorities, with all the risks that were inherent in doing so? What motives could they have had for passing off such a deception?

Is it really conceivable that a religion dedicated to proclaiming the truth about God should have been founded on the basis of a deliberate lie, perpetrated by its founders, about what God had done?

A possibly more plausible variant on the conspiracy theory is that there will have been no deliberate conspiracy, but that rather, very shortly after the death of Jesus, there will have been some false reports that he had been seen alive. As can happen with rumours that are repeated and passed around, these false reports came to be accepted as true among a group of Jesus' followers.

This also seems highly improbable as an explanation of belief in the resurrection of Jesus. The reports would certainly need to have become accepted as true by the leading disciples in particular (Peter, James and John, as the Gospels make clear) before they could have formed the basis for the undoubtedly dangerous proclamation that followed. And is it really likely that they would have been accepted by them without persuasive first-hand evidence that they were true? (The dangers that were involved were ultimately proved, for both Peter and James, by their martyrdoms.)

A series of hallucinations

The hallucination theory may at first sight seem more credible. Individual people can have vivid hallucinations; and hallucinations of seeing and hearing a dead man as though he were alive would certainly seem a real possibility. However, a series of hallucinations involving a number of different people, both separately and together, seems inherently unlikely.

Let us nonetheless suppose a group of people, including the leading disciples, to have had various hallucinations of seeing and hearing Jesus. Let us suppose also that, contrary to what normally happens when people have hallucinations, they were unable to recognise afterwards that this was what they were. Is it really plausible that these entirely deluded men and women would subsequently have been so successful as they were in persuading an increasing number of other people, who themselves had had no such experiences (including several at least of the New Testament authors), that they really had seen and heard Jesus alive after his death?

The resurrection a reality

The third possibility, that Jesus was in truth miraculously raised from death by God, and actually was seen and heard by a number of people on several different occasions, is surely the only one that adequately explains the other facts. It explains why a group of people came to share a belief in this most unlikely happening: because they all shared in similar experiences, which they *knew* could not conceivably have been hallucinations. It explains the start of their dramatic transformation from being a group of demoralised, and almost certainly very frightened, men and women, into a band of people who had the temerity to proclaim that the Jewish authorities – who, a few weeks earlier, had brought about the crucifixion of their own leader as a criminal – had themselves been guilty of executing God's chosen Messiah, who had now been raised to life by God: because they *knew* that what they were proclaiming was true. It explains why the Christian Church was founded: in order that the certain knowledge possessed by these men and women could be proclaimed to the world. And it explains the conviction of the different New Testament authors: because those of them who were not themselves participants in the events must surely have received altogether convincing accounts from those who were.

That the miracle of Jesus' resurrection really did happen, and that he appeared to his disciples more or less as the Gospels describe, is what the Christian Church has always believed. Within the Church the main questioners of the belief as traditionally understood have come from the more radical liberal theologians and scholars, who have general doubts about miracles, and find the idea of a bodily resurrection of Jesus difficult or impossible to accept.

The most extreme radical views have been along the lines that the Church's belief in the resurrection could have stemmed from nothing more than a shared sense among his disciples that, in spite of his death, so powerful were the memories of his life and teaching that his spirit and message lived on with them. It was as though he was still alive – in their hearts he *was* alive. . . As will be apparent, such a view of the origins of belief in the resurrection has certain similarities to the conspiracy theory, and shares much the same implausibility.

For the most part, present-day radical liberal theologians accept that a number of Jesus' close disciples must have had some kind of 'real' experiences, which left them convinced that he had been raised from death by God – although, in their view, these experiences could hardly have been as the Gospels describe. Opinions differ about what may actually have happened: perhaps what the disciples really experienced could have been the spiritual presence of the risen Jesus Christ; or it could have been some kind of God-given vision of his presence, which left them in no doubt that he was alive. Other radical liberals prefer to keep an open mind on how it was that the disciples came to their convictions. In their view there is insufficient evidence to form any definite judgement about what really happened.

Radical liberal views that the actual events, or experiences of the disciples, that gave rise to the belief in the resurrection must in reality have been substantially different from what the Gospels relate can be regarded as implausible, for one particular reason. Whatever actually happened, from the very beginning those who claimed that Jesus had risen from death will undoubtedly have been asked about, and talked about, the events or experiences that gave rise to their conviction, and they will have described them as best they could. In the next chapter we will be considering two specific experiences of the unseen divine presence, both described by Luke in the book of Acts. If, let us assume, the disciples' experiences had been something similar to one or other of these later experiences, they would surely have described them in some such terms as we find in Acts.

Whatever were the original descriptions the disciples gave, we can be sure that these descriptions will have been repeated quite frequently, and passed on, and in due course will have become an important part of the young Church's oral tradition. Any view that what actually happened must have been radically different from the Gospel descriptions involves the presumption that, at some stage, the original descriptions of these crucial events will have become forgotten, or deliberately ignored – to be replaced by the imaginative descriptions (as they are taken to be) that we now have in the Gospels.

There is the highest probability that, at least in the main, the Gospel accounts of the resurrection events are not imaginative creations, but are derived from preserved memories, whether those of first-hand witnesses or oral tradition.

If we accept that the miracle of the resurrection really happened, and that the events surrounding it were more or less as the Gospels relate, there are two more specific questions that still remain. First, was it the actual physical body of the resurrected Jesus that the disciples saw; or was it perhaps some kind of ghostly manifestation of him? And second, why it is that none of the Gospel accounts of the resurrection events agree with one another? No two of them altogether agree in their accounts of the first visits to Jesus' empty tomb. And no two of them give the same, or closely similar, accounts of Jesus' resurrected appearances.

As regards the nature of Jesus' resurrected body, I do not doubt that the disciples saw and heard the real bodily Jesus, not some ghostly manifestation of him. As certain of the accounts seem at pains to stress, it was in some way his 'same' physical body that they saw, and sometimes touched. But it could not have been an entirely normal body he now possessed; for it was evidently one that could miraculously appear and disappear. And, as we are told, there were some occasions when he was not at first recognised. We can perhaps best think of his resurrected body as a miraculously recreated body, which was both similar to and different from his previous body.

The differences between the accounts of the first visit to Jesus' empty tomb could stem from the Gospel authors having used different sources. Alternatively, as some scholars think, Matthew and Luke, and possibly John too, could have based their accounts on Mark, but reshaped them to a certain extent for their own purposes. Either way, there is no reason to think that the accounts do not conform with our general view of the Gospels, that what we are told is likely to be factual in its main substance, but often not in every detail.

As regards the resurrection appearances, the reasons why we have a number of different stories must almost certainly be because they describe what were in fact different appearances. For, as is made clear in the two principal references to the resurrection appearances outside the Gospels, he was seen not just once or twice, but a number of times.

In a letter to the Corinthian churches, which was written about 55 AD, the apostle St Paul (who was not himself one of the original disciples of Jesus, or a witness to the resurrection) makes it clear that he has been told of a number of different appearances.

> For what I received I passed on to you as of first importance . . . that he was raised on the third day . . . and that he appeared to Peter, and then to the Twelve. After that, he appeared to more than five hundred of the brothers at the same time, most of whom are still living, though some have fallen asleep. Then he appeared to James, then to all the apostles. . .
> *(1 Corinthians 15.3–7, NIV)*

The reference here to Jesus having appeared to 'more than five hundred' is something of a puzzle. Some scholars believe it must relate to a resurrection appearance to a large crowd of people not mentioned anywhere else; others think it could be meant as a reference to the coming of the Holy Spirit, described in the next chapter, although it is very unlikely that this event will directly have involved so large a number of people. This puzzle apart, Paul's letter shows beyond any doubt that accounts of resurrection appearances were in fact an important part of the young Church's oral tradition, from well before the Gospels were written.

The other main reference to the resurrection appearances is in the first chapter of Acts.

> For forty days after his death he appeared to them [the apostles] many times in ways that proved beyond doubt that he was alive. They saw him, and he talked with them. . . *(Acts 1.3, GNB)*

The biblical evidence of Jesus' resurrection does not end with the experiences of his disciples immediately following his death, but this takes us into the next chapter.

CHAPTER 7

Some Events that Followed the Resurrection

IN this chapter we will look at what were the three most significant events for the emerging Christian Church within the period immediately following the death and resurrection of Jesus Christ. Each of them had a supernatural content. The first, which came at the end of Jesus' final bodily appearance to his closest disciples, was the occurrence we call the ascension. The second, no more than a week or two later, is known as the coming of the Holy Spirit. The third, which happened several years later, was the conversion of St Paul.

The ascension of Jesus Christ

He ascended into heaven. (Apostles' Creed)

In the opening chapter of Acts, Luke gives us a short description of Jesus' ascension when, some weeks after his death and resurrection, 'he was taken up to heaven' *(Acts 1.2, NIV)* while his disciples were watching. This happened just after he had given them his final instructions:

> 'You will receive power when the Holy Spirit comes on you; and you will be my witnesses in Jerusalem, and in all Judea and Samaria, and to the ends of the earth.' *(Acts 1.8, NIV)*

The account of the ascension reads simply:

> After he said this, he was taken up before their very eyes, and a cloud hid him from their sight. *(Acts 1.9, NIV)*

The narrative then continues:

> They were looking intently up into the sky as he was going, when suddenly two men dressed in white stood beside them. 'Men of Galilee', they said, 'why do you stand here looking into the sky? This same Jesus,

who has been taken from you into heaven, will come back in the same way you have seen him go into heaven.' *(Acts 1.10–11, NIV)*

What are we to make of this account? Did something like the disappearance of Jesus into the clouds, followed by the appearance of two angels, actually happen? Or, as radical liberal theologians have been inclined to think, is the story essentially fictional, and intended to be symbolic of the Christian conviction about the present divinity of Jesus Christ?

Luke's description must I think have at least some factual basis. For if we accept that the resurrection appearances really happened, there must have been a final occasion on which Jesus was seen by his disciples. And it will surely then have been made clear to them that this was to be the last time they would see him in person.

Whether or not there was an actual appearance of angels, what it seems must also have happened is that, through what they understood as a divine revelation, the disciples were left with the certain assurance that thereafter Jesus would be with his Father in heaven. One day, however, he would in some way come back again.

The coming of the Holy Spirit

The next notable event, the coming of the Holy Spirit, happened not many days later, on the morning of the Jewish festival of Pentecost, while the disciples were still gathered together in Jerusalem. The Acts account reads:

> When the day of Pentecost came, they were all together in one place. Suddenly a sound like the blowing of a violent wind came from heaven and filled the whole house where they were sitting. They saw what seemed to be tongues of fire that separated and came to rest on each of them. All of them were filled with the Holy Spirit and began to speak in other tongues as the Spirit enabled them. *(Acts 2.1–4, NIV)*

Once again there are some different opinions among Christian theologians about what may have happened, and about the extent to which the account in Acts can be regarded as factual. However, I think we can best understand what is likely to have taken place in the light of subsequent Christian religious experiences, such as that of John Wesley and his companions in Fetter Lane Chapel, described in chapter 2.

Up to this time the disciples had known Jesus Christ as a man; and after his death they had encountered his visible presence among them. But what they now experienced was something much more: the unmistakable presence of the unseen Divine Spirit. This must have been an overwhelming and transforming experience. And its immediate effect was to give them the certain knowledge that God himself was with those who recognised Jesus as the Messiah. It was on the strength of this certain knowledge and assurance that, as we are told, their leader, Peter, went out immediately to proclaim the news of Jesus' resurrection, with all that it implied *(Acts 2.14-36)*.

Later on in Acts, there are some other references to Christian believers 'receiving' the Holy Spirit, or to the Holy Spirit 'coming on' them *(Acts 8.15–17; 10.44–47; 19.1–6)*. These descriptions may well relate to experiences of a similar nature.

As to what the author meant, in the passage quoted above, by the people present beginning to speak in 'other tongues', this is not altogether certain. If we take the immediately following passage at its face value, they were miraculously enabled to speak in foreign languages they had never learnt. For, as we are told, there were people from foreign lands who were staying in Jerusalem at the time; and they were amazed to hear the disciples speaking in their own native languages. A number of modern theologians think that this is unlikely to have happened, however, and understand Luke's account as referring to the first example of the phenomenon of 'speaking in tongues', which was evidently not uncommon in the early Church.

Speaking in tongues – the technical term is 'glossolalia' – means the uttering, commonly by those who are in the grip of strong religious emotion, of strange and more or less unintelligible 'words' or sounds. It is by no means uncommon today among certain groups of Christians. Sometimes, it appears to have been a consequence of the 'intoxicating' effects of experiencing the reality of the Divine Spirit. On other occasions it may signify no more than a spontaneous boiling over of deep emotions. It can also be a more or less deliberately chosen way of expressing feelings of praise to God, when ordinary language seems inadequate.

The conversion of St Paul

The third notable event took place several years later. During the intervening period, the number of believers had grown considerably. However, an uneasy peace with the Jewish authorities had recently come to an end, and followers of the Way, as they had come to be known – they were not yet called Christians – were now being subjected to a violent persecution. This had started when one of the infant Church's leaders, called Stephen, had been taken before the Jewish council, had enraged its members with a defiant speech, and had then been dragged out to be stoned to death. Following this first Christian martyrdom, a good many other believers, both men and women, had been taken from their homes and put into prison.

Among those who were taking a leading part in the persecution was a man named Saul.

Sometime after the death of Stephen, Saul set out with some companions to go from Jerusalem to Damascus. The intention was to arrest some of the believers there, and to bring them back to Jerusalem for imprisonment. But towards the end of their outward journey, something remarkable happened. We can read the following account in Acts.

> As Saul was coming near the city of Damascus, suddenly a light from the sky flashed round him. He fell to the ground and heard a voice saying to him, 'Saul, Saul! Why do you persecute me?'
>
> 'Who are you Lord?' he asked.
>
> 'I am Jesus, whom you persecute', the voice said. 'But get up and go into the city where you will be told what you must do.'
>
> The men who were travelling with Saul had stopped, not saying a word; they heard the voice, but could not see anyone. Saul got up from the ground and opened his eyes, but could not see a thing. So they took him by the hand and led him into Damascus. For three days he was not able to see. . . *(Acts 9.3–9, GNB)*

As a direct result of this experience, Saul was converted to Christianity. And during the rest of his life, under the adopted name of Paul, he was to become the most outstanding and influential of all the Christian missionary-apostles.

Again we must ask, what actually happened when Paul was on the road to Damascus?

Some Events that Followed the Resurrection

As with other statements that someone has had an experience of a divine presence, there are broadly three possible explanations for the account of Paul's conversion. One is that he, or perhaps someone else, invented the story – maybe with the object of dramatising the importance of his conversion, which was in fact, on this assumption, nothing more than a radical change of heart and mind. The second is that, on his way to Damascus, Paul had an 'experience' similar to that described, but that it was actually some kind of hallucination. The third is that he really did experience the spiritual presence of the risen Jesus Christ.

We can start by ruling out the possibility that the story was invented, either by Paul or by someone else. No one who has carefully read Paul's Epistles could seriously imagine him being a deliberate liar. The strength of his inner conviction is self-evident from the way that he writes. And since he refers a number of times to his 'calling' by Jesus Christ, including a specific mention of Christ having 'appeared' to him *(1 Corinthians 15.8)*, the story told in Acts could hardly be someone else's invention.

But could he not have had a vivid hallucination, with the story about his companions hearing the voice having no historical foundation?

An hallucination can seem very real at the time; but afterwards, assuming that the mind returns to normality, the person concerned usually recognises that the experience was not a 'real' one, but was just 'in the mind'. Only someone whose mind remains seriously disturbed – someone who is more or less permanently deluded – is likely to remain convinced that an hallucinatory experience was a real one. Could Paul have remained deluded in this way for the rest of his life? From all that we can judge of his character from his own letters, it is hard to conceive that a man of such intelligence, insight and wisdom could have been totally mistaken about the nature of the experience that transformed his life.

Luke, who wrote The Acts of the Apostles, must have come to know Paul quite well; for they were evidently companions for some considerable time in Paul's later life. It is clear from the way that he writes about him that Luke can have been in no doubt about the reality of what happened on the way to Damascus. Besides this, over the years that followed his conversion, Paul gained the highest possible standing within the young Christian Church. For this to have happened, the judgement that he was not deluded about the nature of his experience must have been shared among the Church leaders of his time.

Though the alternative views I have mentioned about the nature of Paul's conversion experience have had some supporters, I see no good reason to have doubts about what were manifestly both the conviction of Paul himself, and the judgement of his own closest contemporaries.

In the context of Paul's experience on the road to Damascus, I should add that from the evidence of Christian literature subsequent to the Bible it would certainly appear that other Christians have experienced, in a variety of ways, the spiritual presence of the risen Jesus Christ.

A postscript: an account of a present-day miracle

It remains for me to add the following account of a relatively recent miracle. I give it here because it could have some bearing on our understanding of the events in Jerusalem that immediately followed the coming of the Holy Spirit, described earlier in this chapter, when those who had just shared the experience 'began to speak in other tongues as the Spirit enabled them' *(Acts 2.4, NIV)*.

The account appeared in the 16th September 1994 edition of the *Church Times*, the leading weekly periodical concerned with the affairs of the Church of England, in one of its then regular feature articles about the ministry of individual Christians.

The subject of the article was a Jewish-born London vicar, Ralph Goldenberg, who had been ordained into the Church of England a few years previously. I will summarise the greater part of it.

Ralph Goldenberg had been born into an Orthodox Jewish family, then living in the Sudan; and he grew up able to speak several different languages, including Arabic. Later on the family moved to England, where Ralph completed his education. In due course he married a 'nominal' Christian and started his own family, while working successfully as an ophthalmic optician in Bournemouth.

In the meantime, he had gradually drifted away from his Jewish faith. But then, after a period in a kind of spiritual vacuum, he and his wife joined an Anglican church, to which they were introduced through having made friends with some committed Christians. As time went on they both became increasingly active members of their church.

After a further time, Ralph felt drawn to offer himself for ordination, and was accepted for training. However, towards the end of his period at theological college in Bristol, he started to have serious qualms about what he was doing, and to wonder whether he should be ordained at all.

At this point the *Church Times* article continued by quoting his own words:

> Then, during a college mission, something incredible happened. I hadn't told anyone on the team about my doubts; but one evening the leader said: 'We must lay hands on you because God has something to say to you.' And he gave me a prophetic message in Sudanese Arabic: 'My beloved son, I have called you, you are from the blood, the line of Abraham. I have called you into ministry. The Lord loves you.'
>
> This man didn't speak Arabic, and he thought he was speaking in tongues. To this day, I wonder why God should produce this miracle just for me.

I have recently been in touch with Ralph Goldenberg, who is now the vicar of a parish near Shrewsbury, and he has confirmed the accuracy of what I have written here.

Chapter 8

The Future Return of Jesus Christ

He will come again in glory to judge the living and the dead. (Nicene Creed)

THESE words of the Nicene Creed, which are closely mirrored in the Apostles' Creed, express the Christian conviction that sometime in the future Jesus Christ will return to the world in an unmistakable fashion. His return will be linked with a 'day of judgement', and also, as the Church has generally believed, with the final termination of this present age.

This prophesied return of Jesus Christ is often referred to as the second coming. The theological term for it is 'parousia', from the Greek word meaning 'arrival'.

How was it that the Church came to hold this belief in Jesus' future return? And what are we to make of it today?

The probable origins of the belief can be discerned, first, from certain passages in the Gospels, and second, from the opening chapter of Acts.

In the Gospels of Matthew, Mark and Luke, there are records of Jesus himself making certain prophecies about the future coming of the Son of Man, on a day that will be one of great significance for the world.

> For as lightning that comes from the east is visible even in the west, so will be the coming of the Son of Man... At that time the sign of the Son of Man will appear in the sky, and all the nations of the earth will mourn. They will see the Son of Man coming on the clouds in the sky, with power and great glory. *(Matthew 24.27, 30, NIV; see also Mark 13.26, and Luke 17.24 and 21.27.)*

These prophecies of Jesus, which are further elaborated in adjacent verses, have generally been understood as foretelling his own future return; for, as the Gospels make clear, he quite frequently referred to himself as the Son of Man. (What Jesus may have meant by using this title is discussed on page 69 below.)

Second, quite apart from Jesus' own prophecies, there is the passage already quoted in the previous chapter in connection with his ascension. Here, we read about the angels who appeared to the apostles, saying:

> 'This same Jesus, who has been taken from you into heaven, will come back in the same way you have seen him go into heaven.' *(Acts 1.11 NIV)*

If we take these different texts as having a factual basis – if they give us at least partially true records respectively of what Jesus said, and of what happened at his ascension – then the belief in his future return must have had a dual origin. First, there were his own prophecies, as they were remembered and interpreted by his disciples. And second, there was some kind of divine revelation to the apostles, on the occasion of his ascension.

In more recent years, however, there have been various different opinions among theologians about how Jesus' own prophecies, and the passage in Acts, should be understood, and about how we should regard the belief in his future return. Particularly among radical liberals, there have been general doubts about the literal truth of the Church's traditional belief in the second coming. Scholars and theologians of this school see the whole passage in Acts describing the events surrounding Jesus' ascension as creative story-telling, reflecting beliefs that the Church had previously come to hold. Those who are of this view commonly also believe that Jesus himself must have been mistaken in his expectations about his future return; or alternatively, that his disciples must have misunderstood his prophecies, which were really meant to refer in an oblique way either to his own resurrection, or to the coming of the Holy Spirit.

Despite these differences of view, theologians of all persuasions are widely agreed that within the early Church there was in fact an expectation that Jesus would return. And at least during the first twenty or thirty years, the belief was that his return would not be long delayed. The evidence that there was this expectation is to be found in various passages in the books of the New Testament, notably in a number of Epistles. For example:

> Be patient, then, brothers, until the Lord's coming. . . Be patient and stand firm, because the Lord's coming is near. *(James 5.7–8, NIV)*
>
> The end of all things is near. Therefore be clear-minded and self controlled so that you can pray. *(1 Peter 4.7, NIV)*

(For further examples, see *1 Corinthians 7.29–31, 1 Thessalonians 4.15–17, Hebrews 10.25, 37*.)

As we now know, the belief that Jesus' return would be soon was a mistaken one. This fact has seemed to lend weight to the opinions of those who regard the whole belief, as traditionally understood within the Church, to be misconceived. However, it would be wrong to conclude that, because early Christians were mistaken about how soon Jesus would return, they must have been mistaken in their entire belief. The mistake about when it would be could be attributed in part to some misunderstanding of what Jesus had said; for much that he taught appears not to have been immediately clear as to its precise meaning. Moreover, there is evidence that among the Jewish people at that time there were already expectations of an imminent act of divine intervention to bring their present evil age to an end.

Another confusing factor could have been the recollection of an Old Testament prophecy *(Joel 2.28–32)*, quoted in Acts, which linked the coming of the Holy Spirit with the 'last days', and the 'great and glorious day of the Lord' *(Acts 2.16–21)*. With Joel's prophecy in mind, what happened on that day of Pentecost not long after the ascension could well have been taken as confirmation that Jesus' return would be quite soon.

While a mistake about when it would be appears fairly understandable, a mistake about the entire belief seems most unlikely. It is hard to imagine that the Church leaders would have held, and persisted in holding, the belief unless they were convinced that it was well founded. And there is no good reason to reject the view that its principal foundations were neither Jewish expectations nor the prophecy of Joel, but were in fact the apostles' recollection of what Jesus himself had said, reinforced by some kind of divine revelation on the occasion we know of as his ascension.

As regards what happened at the ascension, given that the whole occurrence was a supernatural one, it is not difficult to believe that it was also the occasion for such a revelation. This is what Luke must have intended us to understand from the description he has given us.

There is thus very good reason to uphold the Church's belief that, in due course of time, Jesus Christ really will 'come again', with all that that momentous event will signify.

CHAPTER 9

The Virgin Birth of Jesus Christ, a Relatively Late Belief

He was conceived by the power of the Holy Spirit and born of the Virgin Mary. (Apostles' Creed)
By the power of the Holy Spirit he became incarnate of the Virgin Mary, and was made man. (Nicene Creed)

THE 'virgin birth' of Jesus Christ, as it is usually called, but more accurately his virginal conception, has been one of the central beliefs of the Christian faith from sometime in the second half of the first century. Unlike the resurrection, however, it was evidently not a belief that was proclaimed in the earliest years of the Church.

How was it that the Church came to hold this belief? Was there really a miraculous birth? Or, as some Christians today are inclined to believe, are the stories about Jesus' birth simply pious legends, which the Church in due course mistakenly came to accept as being the historical truth?

Let us start with what we can learn from the New Testament.

Though the surrounding events that they each choose to describe are different, both Matthew and Luke tell us about Jesus' miraculous conception, through the Holy Spirit, before his mother Mary was married to Joseph *(Matthew 1.18–25; Luke 1.26–38)*. In no other book in the New Testament, however, is there any clear reference to the conception or birth of Jesus. Certainly he is referred to quite often as being the Son of God. But at the time the books were written this description was evidently capable of being understood in more than one way; and it did not necessarily imply that God was his father in the sense that he miraculously caused Mary to conceive.†

† For other meanings of Son of God, see pages 69-70 below.

Matthew's and Luke's Gospels were probably not published until sometime after 75 AD – during the 80s is the most common view – whereas Mark's Gospel was probably ten or fifteen years earlier, and a number of the Epistles were earlier still, from about 50 AD onwards. From the absence of any reference to the birth of Jesus in any of these earlier writings, combined with the absence of reference to it in Acts, which gives a number of accounts of the Christian 'message' that was first proclaimed, it seems reasonable to conclude (as New Testament scholars have generally done) that the miraculous conception of Jesus will not have been part of the originally proclaimed Christian message.

We cannot know for certain how it was that Matthew and Luke came in due course to include their stories about the miraculous birth of Jesus and its surrounding events. Broadly there appear to be three possible alternative explanations. One is that, whatever their original source or sources, the stories were entirely imaginative, but that Matthew and Luke believed them to be true and brought them into their Gospels in this mistaken belief. The second is that, whether the stories were created by themselves or someone else previously, they knew them to be unhistorical, but included them for their symbolic value or for some similar reason. The third, leaving aside the question of whether the surrounding events they describe are historical, is that the central story of the virgin birth itself was known to be true, and had been learnt in the first instance from Mary, or perhaps Joseph, or both. (There are however grounds for believing that Joseph died during the lifetime of Jesus. *See John 19.26–27.*)

The first alternative – that the stories were entirely imaginative, but were believed by the Gospel authors to be true – seems very unlikely. Over the years before the Gospels were written, it should not have been difficult for their authors to find out whether the virgin birth story in particular had originated from Mary (or Joseph), or from some other source, and they would hardly have allowed themselves to remain in ignorance. Luke was certainly in touch with some of the earliest Church leaders.

The second alternative, that both Matthew and Luke included the stories knowing them to be unhistorical, also seems unlikely – particularly if, as I have argued earlier, it was the general intention of the authors to write essentially historical accounts of Jesus' life.

There is a further reason why it is unlikely that the virgin birth story will have had no historical foundation. It is that, throughout the known history of the Christian Church, its leaders have been zealous to stand up for what they believed to be the truths of the Christian message, and to fight against what they have seen to be false beliefs. There is no reason to think that it could have been different in the second half of the first century when the Gospels were published. The leaders of the Church at the time (though we do not know just who they were), like the Gospel authors themselves, will almost certainly have known whether or not the story was authentic – whether or not it had in fact come from Mary (or Joseph). And if it was known not to be true, it is hard to imagine that what had been written by Matthew and Luke would not have been denounced as false; in which case, it is hard to see how the two Gospels could ever have gained the widespread acceptance within the early Church that they clearly did gain.

This fact that the two Gospels did gain widespread acceptance within the early Church is fairly strong evidence that, at the time they were first published, the story of Jesus' miraculous conception was known, among the Church's leaders at least, to be a true one.

There are nonetheless an appreciable number of radical liberal New Testament scholars and theologians who take a different view, and who see Matthew's and Luke's accounts of Jesus' miraculous conception, along with their surrounding stories, as the products of creative imagination. There have been a variety of suggestions about just how the stories may have originated. I will outline just two of them.

In one such view, what Matthew and Luke give us are imaginative stories that are primarily designed to introduce their Gospels by addressing the question 'who was Jesus?' Their essential purpose is to make it clear that the spirit of God rested upon him in a unique degree. Both accounts, which are works of great artistry, contain a number of resonances of stories and passages in the Old Testament, which would be appreciated by many of their first readers. It is doubtful whether the authors ever intended their Gospel introductions to be understood as being historical; it was the later mistake of the Church to regard them as such.

In another rather different view, the central story of the virgin birth is thought likely to have stemmed from the now well-known prophecy of Isaiah.

> The virgin will be with child and will give birth to a son, and will call him Immanuel. *(Isaiah 7.14, NIV)*

(It should be noted that some Bibles have 'young woman' instead of 'virgin'. 'Young woman' is the more normal translation of the Hebrew text word *alma*. However the Greek Septuagint version of the Old Testament, which will have been the one most familiar to the early Christian Church, uses the word *parthenos*, which is correctly translated as 'virgin'.)

The early Church certainly saw Isaiah's prophecy, in the Greek Septuagint version, as applying to Mary and Jesus. As Matthew's Gospel states, after describing how the birth of Jesus came about:

> All this took place to fulfil what the Lord had said through the prophet: 'The virgin will be with child and will give birth to a son, and they will call him Immanuel' – which means, 'God with us'. *(Matthew 1.22–23, NIV)*

As is seen by a number of scholars today, the assumption will naturally have been made within the Church that the prophecy had been fulfilled; and no confirmation from Mary would have been thought necessary, or sought. The birth stories would have been created on the basis of this assumption.

How is the ordinary questioning person to decide between the conflicting views of theologians and scholars about the stories of the virgin birth? There are three main factors that may govern the judgements we personally make: our views about the likely intentions of the Gospel authors; our views about the likely concerns of the Church leaders at the time the Gospels were first published; and our general views on the question of miracles.

In my own judgement, both Mathew and Luke will have been primarily concerned to record historical facts about Jesus, so far as they could ascertain them. It is unlikely that they would have thought it right to start gospel accounts that were intended to be essentially factual with stories that were fictional, but were presented as factual. I also believe that the Church leaders of the day would not have remained silent, if the Gospels contained stories of such importance which they knew were not historical, but would be widely read as historical. Nor would they have been prepared to accept the belief in the virgin birth without the knowledge of Mary's confirmation, simply on the assumption that the prophecy of Isaiah must have been fulfilled. It is much more likely that the prophecy was only seen as applying to Jesus after the fact of his miraculous conception was known.

In the end, however, it will probably be our personal view on the question of miracles that will mainly govern the judgement we make. If you yourself think it very unlikely that Jesus' conception could have been a miraculous one, as the Gospels state, you may well be inclined to accept an explanation of the belief along the lines suggested by radical liberals. But for anyone who believes in the possibility of real miracles, there is no good reason to think that this particular miracle did not happen; rather, there are good reasons to believe that it did.

As for Matthew's and Luke's stories of the various events surrounding Jesus' birth, it is impossible to know for sure to what extent they are factual. There is no independent evidence of any of the events, beyond what we are told in the Gospels. Radical liberals tend to see the stories as imaginative – except, in many views, for the fact that Jesus was born, or at least conceived, before Mary was married to Joseph. For conservative liberals, perhaps the best guess is that long-preserved memories may to some extent have been supplemented by the authors' imagination. I would only add that, for anyone who is inclined to accept that angels do exist, and on occasions have become involved in the affairs of our world, it is entirely reasonable to believe the Gospel accounts of their involvement in the events surrounding the conception and birth of Jesus Christ have a factual basis. For if angels do from time to time play some part in the affairs of our world, the conception and birth of Jesus seem very likely to have been such occasions.

If we accept the story of Jesus' miraculous conception as being true, we are left with the question of why it is that there is no reference to it in any of the earlier New Testament books. The most likely answer is that

The Virgin Birth of Jesus Christ, a Reletively Late Belief

there will have been a period, and probably quite a long period, during which the fact was not widely proclaimed.

From what we are told in Acts, when the Christian gospel message was first proclaimed a few weeks after the resurrection, the central truth that was announced by the leading apostle, Peter, was that the Jesus who had just been crucified was God's chosen Messiah, and that his resurrection was the proof of this *(Acts 2.22–36)*.

The likelihood is that none of Jesus' disciples will have known anything about his conception during his lifetime. He himself would probably not have told any of them. If he had spoken about it, the Gospels would probably have mentioned it; and he could well have judged that the disciples would be unable to take it in, and understand its significance, until after his death and resurrection. Equally, Mary would hardly have thought it appropriate to say anything to them if Jesus himself had chosen not to do so. But after his resurrection, she must sooner or later have thought it right to tell one or two of them.

When in due course the new facts did become known, it will have been only to a small inner circle of Church leaders initially. It is not hard to imagine that they will then have been faced with a dilemma about how and when to make the news more widely known. The gospel of Jesus Christ was being proclaimed on the basis of his resurrection; but while some were accepting it, there were many who were not prepared to believe it. Although among those who were already Christians the news of his miraculous conception might be accepted by most as further confirmation of his unique relationship with God, it would be unlikely to help acceptance of the Christian message among those who were not yet believers.

In the outcome, a number of years must have elapsed before this additional extra-ordinary truth was judged suitable for open proclamation.

CHAPTER 10

The Divinity of Jesus Christ

He ... is seated at the right hand of the Father. (Apostles' Creed)
We believe in one Lord, Jesus Christ ... true God from true God ... of one Being with the Father. (Nicene Creed)

WITHIN the early Church, it was natural that the question should present itself: who was, and is, Jesus? For clearly – in the light of the exceptional quality of his life; in the light of his resurrection and subsequent ascension; in the light of his expected future return; in the light of the knowledge the Church came to have of his miraculous conception; in the light of St Paul's experience, and perhaps also that of others unknown to us, of his spiritual presence in the world – he was, and is, no ordinary man!

The answers to which the Church came, in the course of the first half-century or so following Jesus' death – answers we can find expressed in the New Testament books written during this period – were ones that together accorded to him a divine status, as well as a human one. First, he was recognised as the Messiah, or Christ. The title Christ is taken from the Greek word Christos, which is the translation of the Hebrew word Messiah, meaning in a literal sense the 'anointed one', or more generally a king. Second, he was recognised as Son of God. Third, he was recognised as 'Lord'. And fourth, he was recognised as a fully divine being, who already existed before his life on earth.

Not all Christians today are persuaded that the conclusions the Church came to are right. But let us look more closely at what these conclusions were. We can then turn to the areas where views have differed.

Jesus as Messiah

With little doubt the first answer the young Church came to was that Jesus was the Messiah, the one sent by God, whose coming had been foretold over the previous centuries by a number of the leading prophets of Israel.

Until towards the end of his ministry, Jesus himself had evidently been careful to avoid any direct claim that he was the Messiah. Rather, as the synoptic Gospels make clear, he referred to himself on occasions as the Son of Man. Just what he meant by using this title is a matter of debate among New Testament scholars. One possibility is that in the Aramaic that Jesus would have spoken the phrase could be used simply as a paraphrase for 'I'; but there are other possible connotations it could have had. In most views today, it would not have been understood as signifying that he was the Messiah. In any event he was not like the Messiah that most Jewish people had then come to hope for – someone who would be a great national leader, as well as a great man of God. Any public admission that he was the Messiah would be bound to raise false expectations. It would surely also have brought to an immediate head his growing conflict with the Jewish authorities.

Sometime in the final months, however, as the first three Gospels all record, Jesus admitted to his closest disciples that he was indeed the Messiah; but the disciples were straightaway instructed to tell no one else *(Matthew 16.13–20; Mark 8.27–30; Luke 9.18–21)*. Then, at the very end of his life, we are told of a similar admission to the Jewish authorities, made when he was being questioned by them after his arrest *(Matthew 26.63–64; Mark 14.61–62; Luke 22.67–70)*. It was in fact this admission, or claim, so outrageous to these authorities, that served as the reason for his execution.

For Jesus' followers, it was of course his resurrection that provided the conclusive evidence that he was the Messiah. Indeed, in the earliest days after his death, it was those who recognised him as the Messiah through the knowledge of his resurrection who joined together to form what in due course became the Christian Church.

Jesus as the Son of God

The title Son of God is ascribed to Jesus in a number of New Testament books, and it must have become well established within the Church before the first of them was written. According to both Matthew and Mark, in their accounts of Jesus' questioning after his arrest to which I have just referred, the title was linked by the Jewish High Priest to that of Messiah. It seems likely that the young Church also will have applied it to him from an early stage.

It is a title that was evidently capable of holding a range of somewhat different meanings. First, it certainly signified a person with a uniquely close relationship with God – which in Jesus' case had been fully demonstrated by everything about his public life, by his resurrection, and by the last great event of his ascension. Second, sooner or later it must also have embraced the recognition of his miraculous conception. And third, the words came to hold clear connotations of his divinity.

Jesus as Lord

Again as we see from the New Testament, a further title the early Church ascribed to Jesus was that of Lord. Like Son of God, this also is a word that was, and is, capable of having more than one meaning. First, it denoted the recognition of Jesus as the master of our own lives – the one whose way we seek to follow. Second, it signified, or at least implied, a recognition of his divinity.

The full divinity, and pre-existence, of Jesus

In several places within the New Testament, we find expressions of the belief that Jesus existed (or, as theologians are apt to say, pre-existed) as a fully divine being, before his human birth. The earliest statements of this belief are in two of Paul's letters – those to the churches at Philippi and Colossus.

> [Jesus Christ], being in very nature God . . . made himself nothing, taking the very nature of a servant. . . *(Philippians 2.6–7, NIV)*

> [Jesus Christ] is the image of the invisible God, the firstborn over all creation. For by him all things were created: things in heaven and on earth, visible and invisible . . . ; all things were created by him and for him. He is before all things, and in him all things hold together. *(Colossians 1.15–17, NIV)*

The best-known statement of Jesus' pre-existent divinity comes in the poetical opening verses of John's Gospel, where Jesus is called 'the Word', which is the English translation of the Greek word 'logos', and can here be understood to mean something like 'divine creative power'.

The Divinity of Jesus Christ

> In the beginning was the Word, and the Word was with God, and the Word was God. He was with God in the beginning. *(John 1.1–2, NIV)*

John's Gospel also gives us certain sayings by Jesus in which he himself appears to be asserting his divine nature *(John 8.58, 10.30, 17.5)*. However, a good many modern theologians and scholars think that parts of John's Gospel, including some of the sayings attributed to Jesus, may not be altogether historical, but rather give us the author's imaginative portrayal of Jesus' real nature. On this view we should discount the sayings of Jesus in John's Gospel as original reasons for the Church's belief in his pre-existent divinity: John was putting into the mouth of Jesus what the Church had come to believe about him.

We have no record of how it was that the New Testament authors, along no doubt with other Church leaders, came to the conclusions they did about Jesus' full divinity and pre-existence, and about his activity in creation referred to in the Epistle to the Colossians. We can only surmise. It is not however hard to see that, apart from memories of anything Jesus himself may have said, for the early Church the 'facts' of his resurrection, of his ascension, of his promised future return, and of his spiritual presence in the world will have signified his present divine nature. This in turn must have been seen to point to his divine pre-existence before his human birth; for divinity in its nature is 'eternal', not something that could have been 'acquired' by Jesus, or bestowed on him, as it were in an instant, at the time of his ascension. The knowledge of his miraculous birth will doubtless also have been seen as supporting the same conclusion – as too must the memories of his unique human life.

As for his activity in creation, this could be seen as linked with his divine pre-existence: he would surely not have been an inactive divine being.

However they were reached, the beliefs that the Church came to hold about Jesus Christ, embracing both his divinity and his 'incarnation' as a human being, were in summary more or less these:

– Jesus Christ existed as the divine Son of God from before the beginning of our physical universe; and he was involved in the work of its creation.

- At length, and in due season, he set aside the fullness of his divinity, in order to become incarnate – to be born as a human baby, and live a human life.
- As a sign of his true origin, his birth came about through miraculous conception by the Holy Spirit in the womb of Mary, who was a virgin, chosen by God to be his human mother.
- In his human life he made known to us by his teaching, and even more through his own example, the way that God wishes us to live. He made known to us also something of God's true nature. He likewise made manifest something of his own inner divine nature.
- In his willing acceptance of death on the cross as the termination of his public ministry, he sacrificed himself (as it came to be seen) for the salvation of mankind.
- In witness to his divine authority, he was raised from death by God, and appeared among his disciples.
- Following his ascension, he resumed once more his full divinity.
- In due course of time, he will come again in his full glory; and his second coming will bring our present age to its end.

For a number of centuries after the New Testament books were written, there were those who continued to pursue their own speculations about the 'person' of Jesus Christ. Some of them came to conclusions that the Church leaders judged to be so clearly erroneous that they had to be denounced as heresies, beliefs contrary to the true doctrines of the Church.

The early heresies about the nature of Jesus Christ took a number of different forms. They largely involved attempts to define his true nature, especially the nature of his divinity, often in what today seem rather abstruse philosophical terms. The issues that were mostly in dispute do not nowadays arouse any very widespread interest. But within the Church at the time, particularly in view of their both confusing and divisive effects, it seemed necessary to take them very seriously.

Broadly speaking the heresies in question were seen either as failing to recognise the true nature of Jesus' divinity, or as failing to recognise his full humanity during his earthly life. Thus according to one view Jesus was just a man who was uniquely energised by the Holy Spirit, and who became in effect the 'adopted' Son of God. And on another view, though fully divine, he was never a true human being, but only acted as if he were.

To counter the heresies that were continuing to emerge, it was not enough to condemn what could not be accepted as the truth: it was also seen necessary to state what the truth must be. So it was that during the fourth century the Church undertook the task of defining in fairly precise terms the divine status of Jesus Christ. One of the main outcomes is what we now know as the Nicene Creed, the relevant section of which is set out below in a modern English translation.

> We believe in one Lord, Jesus Christ,
> the only Son of God,
> eternally begotten of the Father,
> God from God, Light from Light,
> true God from true God,
> begotten, not made,
> of one Being with the Father.
> Through him all things were made.
> For us men and for our salvation
> he came down from heaven;
> by the power of the Holy Spirit
> he became incarnate of the Virgin Mary, and was made man.

There are different views among Christian theologians today on the question of whether the creedal authors have succeeded, within the limitations of human language, in expressing the real truth about the divinity of Jesus Christ. On the one hand there are those who hold that the Church's leaders who drew up the creed were so guided by the Holy Spirit that the truth of the creedal statements is beyond questioning. On the other hand there are those who doubt whether there could have been that certainty of guidance from the Holy Spirit, and who in varying degrees have reservations about the creedal definitions of Jesus' divinity. There are also some who doubt his divinity in any sense.

Those who have substantial doubts about Jesus' divinity – whether pre-existent, present or both – are found primarily within the ranks of radical liberal theologians. As we have seen, the tendency in this school is to question the objective truth of the traditional Christian beliefs about Jesus Christ, from the nature of his resurrection to his virgin birth and the meaning of his future return. This questioning commonly applies also to his divinity, or at least to the nature of his divinity. However there is no uniformity of view on this subject; rather there is a range of views.

At the furthest end of the spectrum are those who see Jesus as no more than a truly remarkable but otherwise normal human being, who was chosen by God to play a uniquely important role as his 'representative'. In traditional terms he was a uniquely important prophet. This more or less coincides with the view of those who count themselves as Unitarians rather than as Christians, and who belong to the Unitarian Church.

There are other modern liberal Christian theologians who question the traditional beliefs about Jesus' divinity, and particularly his pre-existent divinity, but who do not put forward any precise views about what the truth may be. This may itself reflect a degree of either uncertainty or open-mindedness as to where the real truth lies.

Among more conservative liberals, of whom I am one, there can be reservations about the precise terms of the Nicene Creed's definitions of Jesus' divinity. If the true nature of God himself is beyond our knowledge and comprehension, so also must be the true nature of Jesus' divinity in relation to God. However, although we may be uncertain about how to define Jesus' divinity (and uncertain about whether the Nicene Creed defines it correctly), the central Christian belief in Jesus' essential divinity, both present and pre-existent, we do not question. Or perhaps more accurately, if we have at some time questioned it, we are persuaded of its truth, or most probable truth.

I do believe myself that in the human life of Jesus Christ, in some way that no one can fully comprehend, God, or some part of God, truly became man.

Differences in belief among Christians

This is an appropriate stage at which to say something on the general question of differences of belief among Christians.

That there are substantial differences of belief among Christians today will be clear from what I have so far written. These differences really start with differences of view about the Bible: whether or not its authors were so inspired by the Holy Spirit as to be infallible; and for those who do not believe that they were so inspired, the extent to which the Bible's narrative stories are historical or historically based, or entirely imaginative. Almost equally basic is whether or not we personally believe, on general principles, that real miracles are possible. The differences of belief about Jesus Christ that we have been considering do, I think, quite largely stem from differences of view on these two issues.

We will be meeting some further differences of belief in the next main section of the book, about God's purpose and plan in creation. Here one of the main underlying issues is how particular sayings of Jesus, or other Bible passages, should be understood.

Going back to the days of the early Church, there is no evidence of significant differences of belief about the inspiration of the scriptures (they were then believed to be wholly inspired), or about the possibility of miracles (they could certainly happen). So far as we know, belief in the virgin birth appears to have been generally accepted, at least from the time when Matthew's and Luke's Gospels were published. But there were continuing differences on the question of Jesus Christ's divinity. These differences were only more or less resolved when the Nicene Creed as we know it was re-approved at the Church's Council of Chalcedon in 451.

Today, most churchgoing Christians worldwide probably accept the Church's beliefs as stated in the creeds without much question. It is only among people with 'questioning' minds – and you would probably not be reading this book unless you are one of them – that some of the creedal beliefs are rejected, or seriously doubted.

I believe that the Church's traditional beliefs about Jesus Christ are essentially the truth. But there are a significant number of questioning Christians who take a different view; and if you personally think it unlikely that there could ever have been any real miracles, you are likely to be among them.

The issue of miracles apart, it will be clear that the evidence and arguments for holding particular Christian beliefs are stronger in some cases than in others. In no case, however, are the evidence and arguments totally compelling: it is always a matter of judging what is most probably the truth. Inevitably, whatever the subject, when the evidence and arguments are not sufficiently compelling to convince all intelligent people that there is only one possible answer, there will be differences of opinion about what is 'probably' the truth. So it is with Christian beliefs.

Many Christians of course, are not 'questioning' people – or at least not so far as their Christian beliefs are concerned. They believe everything the Bible tells them; or they believe that the Church has been so guided by the Holy Spirit that it cannot be wrong in its principal beliefs; or they simply trust that the Church is right. There is much to be said in favour of this kind of trust. For those who have not learnt to be questioning people, or who do not have the educational background to make their own judgements, a simple trust may be the only possible basis for religious faith.

As questioning people we should not expect to know for certain what is the truth on matters of religious belief. Religious beliefs are concerned with matters that lie on or beyond the frontiers of human knowledge. We should remember that, in terms of every kind of knowledge, the human race is on a journey in which we (or rather our distant ancestors) started in total ignorance. Our journey is still far from complete. At this stage of it, in religious beliefs we have to be content with what we see as most probably the truth.

Our religious beliefs should be a kind of 'working hypothesis' – the best hypothesis we can make – on which to base our lives. What ultimately matters most, however, is not whether the beliefs we come to hold are wholly true, but how we live our lives.

As questioning people, we should not be too much upset that there are other Christians who have come to hold somewhat different beliefs from our own. Equally we should respect whatever different beliefs are sincerely held; and we should do our best to prevent these differences from becoming a source of serious division among Christians. Of course we can continue to debate our differences, provided we do so without animosity.

God's Purpose and Plan in Creation

Chapter 11

The Traditional Christian Beliefs about God's Purpose and Plan in Creation

IN the seven chapters that make up this section of the book, we will be concerned with those aspects of Christian belief that are sometimes grouped together under the heading of 'cosmic theology'. That is to say, we will be discussing the great issues that have to do with God's whole purpose and plan in creation.

The questions we will be addressing include:

- What are the grounds for our Christian belief in life after death?
- How will our life in the next world be affected by the way in which we live our present life?
- What can we understand about the nature of God's ultimate purpose in creation? And what also can we understand of his plan for achieving it?
- Why must there be so much pain and suffering in this present life?
- Why should God keep his presence hidden from us, as he does?

Inevitably, in our discussion of these questions we will to a considerable extent be entering the realms of speculation and hypothesis. We cannot expect total certainty; nor will we find it. We will have to remain content with varying degrees of probability, likelihood and possibility.

In the previous chapters I have referred quite often to what we can learn from the New Testament of the Bible. In this section of the book, though a number of passages from it will be quoted, it will generally be of less help to us. I should explain at the outset why this is so. In brief it is because, though the New Testament books do have a fair amount to say on the various subjects that relate to God's purpose and plan in creation, they do not deal with them in any comprehensive way. What we can discover from the New Testament is much more the beginning of Christian thinking on these subjects than the end of it.

Certainly, this is true of Jesus' teaching recorded in the Gospels. He talked at times about life after death *(e.g. Matthew 22.30–32; Luke 16.22–23)*; and we are told that he referred to a 'day of judgement' *(e.g. Matthew 10.15, 12.36, NIV)* which it appeared would come at 'the end of the age' *(Matthew 13.39–40, 49, NIV, GNB)* and which would be linked with his own future return *(Matthew 25.31–33)*. He also spoke in strong language about the dire consequences of the coming judgement for those who fail to turn away from their sins *(Matthew 13.41–42, 49–50)*. But his teaching covers no more than part, if an important part, of our present field of interest.

In the years that followed the death and resurrection of Jesus, the things he was remembered to have said were pondered and discussed; and, as is apparent, they were pondered and discussed in the light of what could be learnt from the Jewish scriptures (which then embraced the books regarded by Protestant churches today as belonging to the Apocrypha to our Bible, as well as those of the Old Testament). Some other Jewish writings of the first and second century BC, contained in what is now known as the 'Pseudepigrapha', were also of evident influence.

In course of time, as can be seen from Christian writings of the early centuries, there developed the main elements of what we may conveniently call the traditional Christian cosmic theology. This came to embrace a number of more or less interlinked doctrines: the fall of man through the sin of Adam and Eve; man's subsequent redemption, made possible through the life and death of Jesus Christ; a judgement with irreversible consequences after the end of this present life; and a renewed, everlasting life in either heaven or hell as the ultimate destination of all human beings.

In what immediately follows, I will give a simplified summary of the traditional Christian cosmic beliefs, as they were generally accepted by the great majority of Christians, although with some variants in the course of the centuries, up till around the middle of the nineteenth century. Much of this traditional collection of beliefs has become questioned, I think rightly so, during the past century or more, particularly among liberally inclined theologians (both conservative and radical). We will be considering some alternative views on a number of the main subjects involved in the next few chapters. The traditional beliefs nonetheless still have a great many adherents within the worldwide Christian Church, although they might in part be expressed today, among some of those who broadly uphold them, in somewhat different terms from those that I use.

God originally created a spiritual world of angels and archangels to live with him in the heavenly regions. At first they all loved and served him as he intended; but in course of time, some of them became envious of him, and revolted against him. After this revolt had been defeated, the rebel angels, whose chief was Satan, were cast out from heaven into a separate abode, where their own evil natures were allowed to prevail.

God then made our own world, with Adam and Eve as the first man and woman, as recorded in the Old Testament book of Genesis. They lived to begin with as God intended them to do, in full obedience to him. But after a time Satan, as an act of spite against God, tempted them to disobey him and to go their own ways. Thus they fell into sin, no longer living in accordance with God's will; and all later generations of men and women, who are descended from them, came to follow their example. So it was that all the evil and suffering of our present world originated from the first sin of Adam and Eve, who fell from divine grace when they succumbed to temptation by the devil (as Satan generally came to be known).

As a result of this first human disobedience – from which, as was believed, there also came death, for otherwise we would have remained immortal – the souls of everyone stayed after death under the power of the devil, destined to suffer the eternal pains of hell. So it would have remained, were it not for Jesus Christ.

In the fullness of time, by God's will, Jesus Christ came into the world in order to save us from the consequences of Adam's sin. Through his teaching, and through the example of his own life, he has shown us the way back to life as God always intended it to be. But more than this,

The Traditional Christian Beliefs about God's Purpose and Plan in Creation

by his own sacrificial death on the cross, he atoned for the sins of the whole world, and thereby made possible our redemption. That is to say (though there have been some rather different versions of the doctrines of atonement and redemption), through his own suffering and death he paid the full penalty for sin that was hitherto due to be paid by all human beings, in the form of eternal punishment, after death, in hell. As a result of this, God is able to offer forgiveness to all those who repent of their previous sin.

The death of Jesus Christ also earned release for the souls of those who had died previously, but who had led just lives and merited salvation.

The nature of our next life, which will be everlasting, will depend entirely on how we have lived in this present life, particularly on our adherence to the Christian faith. For after we have died, we will all have to face the judgement of God – a judgement that may come either immediately, or on a day of general resurrection linked with the return of Jesus Christ. According to God's judgement on us, we will either be granted eternal salvation and joy in heaven, or we will be condemned to eternal damnation and suffering in hell. In some beliefs, however, those who are ultimately destined for heaven will have to undergo an initial period of suffering in purgatory, whenever this is necessary to purify them of their residual sins.

If we are to be saved from eternal damnation, we must in this life repent of our sins, accept Jesus Christ as our Lord and Saviour, and thereafter seek to live according to God's will. This will ensure our salvation, and admittance into heaven, to live for evermore in the loving presence of God. For everyone else there could be no escape from hell.

During the second half of the nineteenth century, partly as a result of new and more critical approaches to the study of the Bible, and partly also as a result of the growing acceptance of 'Darwinian' theories of evolution, a progressively increasing number of Christians started to question various aspects of these traditional beliefs. Thus, more and more people came to the conviction that, contrary to what had previously been believed, the Genesis stories of the creation of the world, of the origins of man, and of his 'fall' due to temptation by the devil, could not be historically true. There could never have been a time when any human beings lived in a state of perfection and full obedience to God.

From this starting point, liberally inclined theologians were led to reconsider a number of the traditional beliefs. The Genesis story of the fall of man came to be seen as true in some general symbolic sense rather than literally. The revolt of Satan and his rebel angels before the foundation of our world was seen to be a purely mythological idea. A number of theologians also came to question whether Satan, the devil – believed to be a universal spiritual power of evil, able to influence the thoughts and actions of men and women, and the supposed original source of all human evil – really does exist. Rather, it was seen that the origins of human evil could be understood in purely human terms.

Beliefs about the nature of judgement, and its irreversible consequences for the next life in heaven or hell, likewise became subject to reappraisal; for the traditional doctrines were seen to be inconsistent with a new understanding of divine justice, and of God's likely purpose and plan in creation.

The doctrines of atonement, though still accepted in one form or another by many Christians, also became increasingly questioned. The doctrines were originally linked with the belief that, following the first sin of Adam and Eve, all human beings, who inherited their sinfulness, incurred God's wrath and became condemned after death to suffer eternal punishment in hell. Jesus Christ through his death on the cross 'cancelled out' the effects of Adam's and Eve's sin, and secured our redemption from hell by himself paying the full penalty for our sins. If in reality, however, human beings were never created sinless, but evolved from primitive and ignorant beginnings, a just and loving God could surely not have condemned the human race to eternal punishment on that account. The atonement doctrines did not make sense in relation to the new understandings both of our evolutionary human origins, and of what divine justice must entail. A just and loving God could surely never have required the sacrificial death of his Son, as a penalty that had to be paid for all human sin, before it became possible for him to forgive us.

It is true that all human beings, to a greater or lesser extent, are sinful. But, as it increasingly came to be seen, all that is really necessary, or ever was necessary, to obtain God's forgiveness is our own true

The Traditional Christian Beliefs about God's Purpose and Plan in Creation

repentance. The scriptural passages taken to support the traditional atonement doctrines should be understood in some rather different ways (as they certainly can be). What Jesus Christ has really done is to show us the true way of life, and enable all those who acknowledge him to escape from their past sinfulness and follow that way, in reconciliation with God. How has he done this? He has done it through his whole life and teaching, with his death as the culminating event of his life – through his life, teaching and death together, though we may fairly choose to emphasise his death (as the scriptural passages often do). In this way we can truly say that he gave his life, and suffered death on the cross, to enable us to escape from our previous sinfulness, and become reconciled with God.

Where does all this reappraisal leave Christian cosmic theology today? There is no simple answer to that question. Undoubtedly many Christians have come to doubt or reject, or at least to re-express, much of the traditional cosmic theology I have outlined. On the other hand, particularly among Christians who believe in the infallibility of the Bible (probably a still substantial proportion of all Christians worldwide), most if not all of the traditional beliefs could remain broadly accepted. In brief, within this whole area there is a diversity of beliefs – and among many Christians probably also much uncertainty.

In the chapters that follow I will be seeking to explore some of the main issues in the field of Christian cosmic theology, as it were without any preconceived ideas about what our conclusions ought to be. The conclusions that will be reached are ones that I believe will be widely shared, though they might sometimes be expressed a little differently, among liberally inclined theologians today.

Chapter 12

God must have a Purpose and Plan in Creation

IT cannot be proved absolutely that God has a purpose in creation. But everything we have come to understand about God points very strongly to the conclusion that he does have a purpose in creation; that his purpose must be a good one; and that human beings must have an important place in that purpose (though not necessarily the only important place).

Christians see God to be a God of perfect love, perfect justice and infinite wisdom; for the creator of all life must possess, in the highest degree, the qualities we most admire in human beings at their best. That perception apart, God's perfect love has been exemplified, and confirmed for us beyond doubt, through the loving life and death of Jesus Christ, whom we recognise as God's Son, possessing his nature. The perfect justice of God is an essential part of his perfect love. The infinite wisdom of God we can see demonstrated in the amazing works of his creation.

God being as he is, he could not have created the universe other than for some good purpose. We could not really imagine, as an alternative, that the whole universe is just a gigantic experiment, created 'to see what happens' with no ultimate end in view. For so irresponsible an act would be completely alien to God's nature, as we have come to understand it.

It must also be that we ourselves have a very important place in God's purpose. For this is clear both from the facts of Jesus' life, death and resurrection, and from all that he taught.

If God has a purpose, he must surely also have a plan for achieving it; for it could not really be otherwise, with a God of infinite wisdom. And there is a further assumption that more or less follows from this. It is that if we had complete knowledge – the knowledge that God himself must have — everything about the universe would be seen to make good sense, in relation to God's plan.

In our present state of knowledge, there are some aspects of God's creation that, at first sight, do not seem to make any real sense. Why has God, whom we know through Jesus Christ to be a God of perfect love, created a world in which there is so much terrible suffering? How can a God of perfect justice permit so much injustice in the world? Why does a God who, as Jesus taught us, desires our love keep his presence hidden from us?

We may not, at first sight, see sensible answers to these questions. But the reaction of Christian theologians to such puzzles is: if we knew everything, these apparent paradoxes would be resolved. There must be good reasons for the present sufferings of our world; injustices must in the end somehow be remedied; there must be good reasons, too, why God has not revealed himself to all of us.

At present, we can see only a few pieces in the jigsaw puzzle of God's plan; but let us try to envisage something of the fuller picture, of which these pieces must be a part. Of course, with our present limited knowledge, our picture is bound to be a very incomplete one; and we cannot be sure how closely it will correspond with the reality of things. But at least, it may serve to show some possible way or ways in which everything could make sense.

The central Christian belief about God's purpose and plan in creation is that it involves life after death. In the next chapter, we will consider the grounds for this belief.

Chapter 13

Life after Death

I believe in . . . the resurrection of the body, and the life everlasting. (Apostles' Creed)
We look for the resurrection of the dead, and the life of the world to come. (Nicene Creed)

IN this chapter, we start with the basis for our belief in life after death, affirmed in the creedal statements above. We will then go on to consider some other related questions.

Before going any further I should say that, though the Apostles' Creed refers to the resurrection of the 'body', and the traditional Christian belief was that our present physical bodies would be restored to life, probably most Christians today do not have this belief. We generally understand the body to mean a new 'spiritual' body, into which we will be transformed. This is in line with what St Paul has written on the subject.

> When buried, [the body] is a physical body; when raised, it will be a spiritual body. *(1 Corinthians 15.44, GNB)*

The reasons for believing in life after death

Belief in life after death is a belief that Christians have held from the very beginning of the Church. It was already at that time a largely accepted belief within the Jewish religion. But what are the main grounds today for continuing to believe that there really is life beyond death?

There are three main grounds for our belief, on which I will be elaborating. These are:

— The teaching of Jesus points clearly to life after death.
— Our beliefs about God and about his purpose in creation point strongly to the same conclusion.
— Our growing relationship with God confirms this conclusion.

Some people would add, as further grounds for the belief, that there is quite a lot of evidence about 'contacts' of one kind or another with the spirits of dead people. However, since I have made no study of the evidence myself, I will leave it aside.

The teaching of Jesus

In Jesus' time, the majority of Jews believed in life after death, but it was a relatively recent belief within their religion, and it did not feature in the main bulk of their scriptural books, which form our Old Testament. Standing out against the majority, there was a sect known as the Sadducees, who adhered particularly to the traditional core of the Jewish scriptures in which the belief had no place, and who accordingly did not accept it.

From what we are told in the Gospels, Jesus himself clearly had no doubts about life after death. Much of his teaching points forward to a life beyond this one. As an example of this, three of the four Gospels – Matthew, Mark and Luke *(Matthew 22.23–32; Mark 12.18–27; Luke 20.27–38)* – record Jesus' answer when some Sadducees asked him a tongue-in-cheek question about what would happen in the case of a woman who married seven brothers in turn, one dying after the other: which of them would be her husband in the next life? Jesus' answer to them includes the words:

> When the dead rise to life, they will be like angels in heaven and will not marry. *(Matthew 22.30, GNB)*

Even if there may be some doubts about how accurately the Gospels record what Jesus said, there can be no doubt at all that the New Testament authors shared a convinced belief in life after death. This belief must certainly have been grounded in the teaching of Jesus himself, as well as in the mainstream Jewish belief.

Apart from his teaching, many Christians have seen the resurrection of Jesus as further evidence that there must be life after death. As St Paul himself wrote, in the context of discussing our own resurrection:

> But the truth is that Christ has been raised from death, as the guarantee that those who sleep in death will also be raised. *(1 Corinthians 15.20, GNB)*

Our beliefs about God and his purpose in creation
More or less independent of Jesus' teaching, there is another compelling reason for believing that there must be life after death.

Christians know God to be a God of perfect love and absolute justice. But in our present world, as it is today and as it always has been throughout known history, for a great many people injustice and suffering (much of it as far as we can see more or less undeserved suffering) have been the predominant experiences of their lives. How can we reconcile our conviction about God's perfectly loving and just nature with these inescapable facts of widespread undeserved suffering and injustice in this present life? Could a God of absolute love and justice really have created us just for this present life, in which so many people appear to be more or less innocent victims of suffering and injustice? That would simply not appear to make sense.

If God has an ultimate purpose in creation, as we are sure he must have; and if that purpose is a good one, as it must be; and if human beings have an important place in that purpose, as we must have: then it must be that the fulfilment of God's purpose will lie in a future life, in which we will all have a part. It must lie in a future life, because it clearly cannot lie in this one with all its suffering and injustices, and with death as the ultimate fate of every creature.

Though we do not know for certain because there is insufficient surviving evidence, it could well have been somewhat similar reasons that first led Jewish religious thinkers to a belief in life after death (a belief that appears to have become prevalent during the last two or three centuries before the birth of Jesus). If, contrary to the older belief expressed in much of the Old Testament, God did not in fact ensure justice for everyone in this present life – if those who led good lives in accordance with his will all too often were not rewarded as they should be in this life, and those who led evil lives often seemed to go on prospering – then there must be a future life in which the justice of God would finally be upheld.

Our growing relationship with God
There is a further, independent, reason for believing that there must be life after death.

Christians in this life start to build up a real loving relationship with God. Some people progress much further than others in the growth of this relationship, which comes largely through prayer; but even those who appear to have advanced the furthest would not claim to have come anywhere remotely near to knowing the full reality of God's being. Yet – and from what I have read this always seems to be the experience – the further a person advances in the knowledge of God, the greater becomes their awareness of how much more lies ahead.

And so it is that those who have come closest to God have come also to the deepest assurance, the feeling of absolute certainty, that there must be a future life in which they will finally see God face to face.

Is it conceivable that the closer a person comes to God in this life, the more he or she is deceived about the future? Could God have called us to start a journey along a road, if we are never to reach the destination to which that road is signposted? Could there be any sense in God encouraging us to start building up a loving relationship with him, if it only leads . . . to nothing?

It will be clear that, though the reasons for believing in life after death are convincing to Christians, and to some extent similarly to Jews and Muslims, who share a belief in the same God, they will not be at all convincing to atheists or agnostics. For these reasons are essentially related to our beliefs about God.

Alongside the teaching of Jesus, it is our belief in the existence of a loving, wise and purposeful God that leads us to the conviction that there must be life after death. Though there are some exceptions, those who have no belief in God usually see no reason to believe that there could be anything beyond this visible life on earth: belief in life after death, like belief in God, can only be wishful thinking, or vain imagining!

Some related issues
Under this heading there are several questions to be considered, each relating to our 'souls'.

What is our soul?
In present-day Christian belief it is our souls, not our physical bodies, that will survive death. But what is our soul?

We understand the soul to be the 'spirit' of a living person. It must comprise everything that makes us what we are in personality. It is thus our essential being, as we have become in the course of this life. During our life on earth, our souls are linked with our physical bodies. But after death they will assume some new mode of existence.

But can this 'being' that is our soul really be separated from our physical body? Can there be a mind that is capable of consciousness, memory, thought, decision, feeling and communication with other minds, detached from our physical body and brain? Can there really be disembodied spirits?

The Christian answer is that it must certainly be possible for conscious beings to exist in a form that is different from the physical one we know. We cannot imagine what this form will be, simply because it lies altogether outside our experience. (A caterpillar, if it were capable of thought, would surely find it hard to imagine becoming a butterfly!) As we believe in a spiritual God, it is not difficult to believe that we ourselves could exist in a spiritual form. It could well be that in the next life we will have some new kind of bodies; but if so, whether these new bodies, spiritual or otherwise, will have any resemblance to our present bodies we cannot know.

However, there is one assumption we can reasonably make. It is an assumption that is implicit in the very meaning of life after death, as Christians have always understood it. This is the assumption that, in the next life, we will be conscious beings with a clear sense of our own identity; and that, linked with this, our future personalities will in some way be continuations of our present personalities. We will start, in the next life, more or less as we have 'become' in this life. We can expect to know who we are (and this surely implies at least some memory of our present life). And we will in some way be recognised by others, who have known us in this life – as we too will be able to recognise those we have previously known and loved.

Do all human beings have souls that will survive death?
Whatever form the embodiment of our souls may take in the next life, the existence and continuing survival of our souls must lie – as indeed must everything that exists – within the providence of God. There could

be nothing in any form, whether in this world or the next, apart from God.

If the survival of our souls is dependent on the providence of God, this raises the question of whether the souls of every human being will survive death. Does it perhaps depend on whether, in God's eyes, we deserve to survive?

It has always been the prevalent Christian belief that every person is destined for continuing life in the next world, whether in heaven or hell. However, there has been an alternative doctrine, known as 'conditional immortality', which has in the past had a number of adherents. This is the belief that, though every person will face divine judgement after this present life, only those souls that have proved themselves worthy of survival will gain immortality. All other souls will perish, either immediately or after a period of punishment.

For reasons that should become more apparent in the following chapters, I do not think that conditional immortality is a plausible doctrine. Suffice it to say here that it is hard to see how, on the basis of this life alone, a God of perfect love and justice could make a fair and just division between souls that survive and souls that perish.

What about the souls of infant children?

Just how and when our souls come into existence is part of the mystery of life, and the mystery of God. We cannot know at what point, following the conception of a baby, it may first have a soul that, in the providence of God, will survive physical death. In common Christian belief, we all have souls that will survive death from the time of our birth onwards (or from sometime before, in the case of a stillborn baby). I see no reason to doubt this. The soul of an infant child, as with its personality, will inevitably be undeveloped compared with that of an adult; but it can still be capable ultimately of the fullest life in the world to come.

At what point, in the course of evolution, could human beings (or more primitive creatures) have first possessed surviving souls?

If human beings have evolved from more primitive forms of animal life, the question obviously arises: at what point in the course of evolution did living creatures, whether human beings or some form of animal, first possess souls that became capable of surviving physical death? We cannot of course know the answer to this question. But just as there must be a critical point before its birth at which the emerging soul of a child developing within its mother's womb becomes capable of surviving physical death, so there must also have been a point in the progressive course of evolution at which certain living creatures first developed souls capable of surviving their deaths. And much as with the soul of an infant, it can only be that God himself will have determined that point.

We may speculate that it could perhaps have been some point at which a certain group of creatures, living in rather abnormal circumstances, managed to achieve a significant mental or behavioural advance, compared with all previous creatures. But whatever the truth may be, we cannot expect to know it.

Is reincarnation a possibility?

Some people may wonder if there could be truth in the idea of reincarnation – the idea that each of us inherits the soul of some person, or possibly some animal, who has lived and died previously, and that after our own deaths we will be reborn in some other person, or animal. Belief in reincarnation, which has been held mainly by Hindus and Buddhists, is in straight conflict with our Christian conviction that every soul after death will move on to a different kind of world from this one. It is in conflict also, as we will see, with our understanding of God's whole purpose and plan in creation.

In Christian belief, every person's soul is unique to that person, and has no existence before this present life: there can therefore be no place for belief in reincarnation.

What happens to our souls after death is the main subject of the next chapter.

Chapter 14

Judgement, Heaven and Hell: the Consequences for the Next Life of how we Live in this Life

He will come again to judge the living and the dead. (Apostles' Creed)

It has always been the Christian conviction that, after death, we will each of us be judged according to how we have lived our present life. This judgement, we believe, will determine what happens to us in the next life.

There have been different beliefs both about what our judgement will entail and about when it will take place. The Apostles' Creed quoted above, and similarly the Nicene Creed, express the belief that there will be a day of divine judgement for every soul, which will be linked with the return of Jesus Christ and the end of the present age. For all those who have died earlier there will be an interval of 'sleep' until this day. Another belief, also widely held, is that we will each of us face some kind of judgement more or less immediately after death. Some New Testament passages point to the former belief, others to the latter. A further belief held by some, though not generally in the mainstream Christian churches today, is 'millenarianism': linked with the return of Jesus Christ there will be a thousand years of resurrected life for the Christian saints, before the day of general resurrection and judgement comes. This particular belief is based on a fairly literal interpretation of a passage in the book of Revelation *(Revelation 20.1-6)*.

I will not pursue any further the judgement timing question. It does not particularly affect anything else we will be discussing; and however much we might speculate, the true answer must remain beyond our knowledge.

Moving on to what our judgement will entail, as we have seen earlier, the traditional belief is that it will determine for all eternity whether our souls go to heaven or to hell. Those who have led sufficiently good Christian lives will find themselves welcomed into heaven, and into the eternal presence of God. All other souls will be condemned to suffer the unending punishments of hell. In some beliefs, notably those of the Roman Catholic Church, Christians who are destined eventually for heaven, but are still in a state of sinfulness, will first need to undergo a period of purification in purgatory before they can be fit to enter heaven.

In earlier centuries, and certainly in medieval times, both hell and purgatory were believed to be places of physical torment. In hell the torments were unending, but in purgatory they would only be temporary. Present-day beliefs can be rather different. Purgatory is now seen by Roman Catholics very much as a place or time of purification rather than punishment. And, among Christians generally, the miseries of hell tend to be seen as mental more than physical, and the natural consequences of total separation from God. But for those who have beliefs along the traditional lines, whatever the nature of hell there could be no hope of any future escape: anyone who goes to hell will remain there for all eternity.

Among those who question the traditional beliefs about judgement, heaven and hell, what are the main criticisms? And what are seen to be the alternatives?

Leaving open what the real nature of heaven may be, there is no reason to question the belief that the souls of those who have led sufficiently good Christian lives will find themselves in heaven, or at least on the road to heaven. Beliefs along these lines remain generally accepted throughout the Christian Church.

What is rejected by many Christians today is the traditional belief in judgement as entailing a sharp and final division at the end of this life between the souls of the saved and the damned, with the damned (which broadly included all who were not Christians) being consigned to unending punishment in hell. Though those who continue to uphold this traditional belief see it as what the Bible clearly teaches – I will return to that shortly – for other Christians it is incompatible with our belief that God is a God of perfect love and justice.

There could be no true justice in any simple, sharp and final division at the end of this present life between the souls of the saved and the damned. All of us, or nearly all of us, Christians and non-Christians alike, have both good and bad sides to our characters. In some, but in varying degrees, the good predominates, in others the bad. Moreover, how could a God of perfect love and justice choose to condemn, for example, those who have never had any real chance to know about Jesus Christ to some unending punishment?

Divine justice could surely not be satisfied by any sharp and final division of souls at the end of this life.

The original belief in hell as a place of everlasting flames and physical torment, and the partly related belief that there will be a sharp and final division between the souls of the saved and the damned, appear to have been derived in large part from a fairly literal interpretation of certain of Jesus' recorded sayings.

> As the weeds are pulled up and burned in the fire, so it will be at the end of the age. The Son of Man will send out his angels, and they will weed out of his kingdom everything that causes sin and all who do evil. They will throw them into the fiery furnace, where there will be weeping and gnashing of teeth. *(Matthew 13.40–42, NIV)*

> When the Son of Man comes in his glory . . . all the nations will be gathered before him, and he will separate the people one from another as a shepherd separates the sheep from the goats. He will put the sheep on his right and the goats on his left. . . The King . . . will say to those on his left, 'Depart from me, you who are cursed, into the eternal fire prepared for the devil and his angels.' *(Matthew 25.31–33, 40–41, NIV)*

As a good many theologians other than traditionalists now see it, Jesus did really not mean what he said here to be taken altogether literally. Rather, he was using colourful expressions to stress that how we live in this life will undoubtedly have very real and serious consequences for us, good or bad, for the next life.

There was nothing unusual in his speaking in this picturesque and exaggerated kind of way. He quite often used dramatic forms of speech to make the points he wanted to make in ways that were likely to be remembered, but were not to be taken too literally. Let me give another example in a different context:

> If your right eye causes you to sin, gouge it out and throw it away. It is better for you to lose one part of your body than for your whole body to be thrown into hell. And if your right hand causes you to sin, cut it off and throw it away. . . *(Matthew 5.29–30, NIV)*

In the present context we should also bear in mind that at the time the Church's doctrines on judgement were being formulated in the light of Jesus' teaching, conceptions of justice were generally much cruder than they are at their best today. Roman justice was apt to be rough justice.

While we cannot know for certain, the true meaning of judgement seems most likely to be something like this: how we are placed at the beginning of the next life will depend on what our personality has become in this life, which itself will be the result of how we have chosen to live. God's judgement on us will be a 'natural' judgement. What we have become, or failed to become, as a result of how we have lived, will have its natural consequences. The better our souls are fitted for the next life, the better our natural situation in it will be, and vice versa.

If this is indeed so, what do we need to do, to fit ourselves as best we can for the next life? The answer, surely, is that we need to live as best we can according to the Christian understanding of God's will for us – that is, to follow as best we can the Christian way of life. We have to live as nearly as we can in the way that Jesus himself has taught and shown us. The heart of this way is that we should seek to grow in love – using that word in its full Christian sense – both for God and for our fellow human beings.

Of course not many Christians, if any, succeed in living entirely, or even nearly, as ideally as we should. We virtually all of us fail from time to time, and many of us fail frequently. What surely matters is that, however much we may fail, we should keep on trying. We should then have nothing to fear about our coming judgement. Whether or not we have reached our final destination, we will surely find ourselves welcomed into a far better world than this present one.

It would be futile to speculate at any length about what may be the nature of heaven and hell, and about whatever 'purgatory' may lie in between them. The next life is hidden from us behind a kind of impenetrable veil, and we cannot know anything about its real nature. But of one thing we can feel sure, as Christians generally have done: whatever else its nature, heaven will be a place of lasting peace, love and joy. Whereas in hell, there will be neither peace, nor love, nor joy.

As for the immediate outcome of our judgement, this much I think we can expect. The more nearly we become as God wishes us to become, by living now as he wishes us to live – the more nearly we become both loving and lovable – the more we will find ourselves in the next life in the company of other souls that are both loving and lovable; and surely also, the more we will be able to know the reality – a marvellous reality it must be – of God himself.

On the other hand, the more we become the opposite of what God wishes us to become – the more we become unloving and unlovable – the more we will find ourselves either in miserable isolation from other souls or in the company only of other souls that are themselves unloving and unlovable. So too there will be a total separation from God himself. Whatever else may be the nature of hell, something like this will surely be a part of it.

Will this then be the end of it: that once this present life is over, every soul will have to stay wherever it finds itself, according to its judgement, for all eternity – to stay for ever as it has become in this present life, without any further opportunity to change, and to become more nearly as God must wish us to become?

I cannot believe so. The Roman Catholic concept of purgatory surely points to an important truth: there will be a place or time of purification, in which it will be possible for us to overcome our imperfections and move ever closer towards heaven. Indeed, using the traditional terms, there may be no sharp divisions between heaven, purgatory and hell. All souls that have not reached heaven could undergo some suitable combination of purification and 'punishment', in an almost infinite range of possible degrees. And maybe even for the most evil souls there could be the possible eventual prospect of moving progressively from hell, through purgatory, towards heaven.

However, a fuller discussion of what may happen in the next life, and of other related questions, takes us beyond the subject of judgement, and belongs to the next chapter.

Chapter 15

What can we Understand of God's Plan in Creation?

THIS chapter will be exploring some subjects that lie beyond the boundaries of beliefs covered by the Christian creeds, but on which many Christian thinkers have pondered and continue to ponder. The main questions we will be considering are:

— What can we understand of God's ultimate purpose in creation, and of his general plan for achieving it?
— Why has God not simply created us as he wishes us to be?
— What is the place of our present life, in the context of God's whole creative plan? And how in this context should we see the coming of Jesus Christ?
— What happens after this life to souls that have not reached their intended destination in heaven?
— How much does it matter whether or not we live as Christians in this life?

Our understanding of God's ultimate purpose in creation, and of his general plan for achieving it

While we cannot know for certain what is God's ultimate purpose in creation, it is noteworthy that among Christians who have written on this subject there has been a widely shared vision. The vision they have had is that of a final consummation, when at last all conscious beings are united together, with God and with one another, in an eternal communion of perfect love, peace and joy. Paul's Epistle to the Ephesians puts it thus:

> This plan, which God will complete when the time is right, is to bring all creation together, everything in heaven and on earth, with Christ as head. *(Ephesians 1.10, GNB)*

What can we Understand of God's Plan in Creation?

To many people this vision of heaven as a perfect eternity, in which all souls are united for ever in loving and joyful communion with God, may not have very much immediate appeal. This is hardly surprising: we cannot really feel a desire for something that is beyond our present comprehension. A child cannot really understand what it is for a man and woman to be in love! However – and this is the common Christian experience – as we begin to gain some understanding of all that God must be, so does our love for him start to grow, and so does our desire to be in his closer presence.

In this present life the highest kinds of fulfilment we can know are often to be found in close relationships with other human beings. In relationships of love, or of close friendship and mutual understanding, our personalities somehow gain new dimensions, and our whole state of consciousness takes on a higher quality than when we are on our own. If this is true of our human relationships in this present world, will it not be far more true of our relationship with God, when it comes to its fullest fruition?

There may indeed be more to heaven than the unending perfection of our communion with one another and with God, though the joy of that must surely be central to everything else.

If God's purpose in creation (or at least a part of it) is more or less as many Christians have believed it to be, for this purpose to be achieved we ourselves must become fit to have our place in its achievement. What does this require of us? We cannot really know all that it may entail, but the sum of it must be this: that our souls should in the end attain their fullest possible maturity and perfection. And whatever else, this maturity and perfection of our souls must surely entail the perfection of their capacity to form close and loving relationships with other souls, and with God himself. It must likewise also entail the perfection of their lovableness.

God's plan in creation must be aimed at enabling us to achieve the kind of perfection he desires us to achieve. Our present lives on earth should be seen in this context. So also must whatever may lie between the end of our present lives and the final accomplishment of God's purpose.

To understand as much as we can of God's creative plan, we need to start by looking back to its beginnings. After that we can return more briefly to the purpose of our present life, and then look forward to what may lie beyond it, before the final consummation of God's purpose is achieved.

In traditional Christian belief, God made man and woman as he wished them to be; but before long, through the temptation of the devil, they fell into sin, and all subsequent generations of human beings have inherited their sinfulness. As many Christians now believe, the traditional account of man's creation is mythological. Progressive evolution, entailing our own progressive development, is God's chosen method of creation. It would not have been possible for him simply to have created human beings immediately as he wishes us ultimately to be.

Why God could not simply have created us as he wishes us to be

The first two chapters of the Bible tell how God created our world, with Adam and Eve as the first man and woman *(Genesis 1 and 2)*. The account we are given certainly suggests that these first two human beings were created entirely as God wished them to be: he created them 'in his own image', and, as we are told, after he had completed everything in his creation, 'God saw all that he had made, and it was very good' *(Genesis 1.27, 31, NIV)*. Adam and Eve would so have remained, had they not after a time fallen to temptation by the devil *(Genesis 3)*.

That Adam and Eve were originally created as God wished them to be is in any event broadly speaking what the Christian Church in due course came to believe, and continued to believe until comparatively recent times. It was the common belief that the creation and subsequent fall of Adam and Eve were actual historical events.

Worldwide today, particularly among Christians who believe in the inerrancy of the Bible, there are probably still many who hold to the traditional belief in the historical creation of Adam and Eve as the first human beings. But in Britain, and largely throughout the more scientifically knowledgeable world, most people now believe that human beings have evolved progressively from more primitive forms of life, over many millions of years. Among Christian theologians, it is today widely accepted that the Genesis account of creation, and of the subsequent 'fall' of Adam and Eve, should not be regarded as history. Rather, the stories are in the nature of imaginative attempts by early Jewish writers, who could have known nothing of modern sciences and of the theory of evolution, to account for the origins of our universe and world, and of human beings with all their imperfections of nature. Though not historical, the opening chapters of Genesis do nonetheless express some profound religious truths. In particular, they express the truth that everything is ultimately the creation of a single God, and the truth that, although we human beings are God's creation, our present natures are far from perfect, and far from what God wishes them to be.

I see no reason to question the modern view of our evolutionary origins. While there are still very large gaps in our knowledge of what has actually happened, the evidence gathered over the last century or so that higher forms of life must have emerged through long processes of gradual change and development, starting from very simple forms of life, seems now to be overwhelming. Evolution, as I have said, is God's chosen method of creation.

We have no means of knowing whether God may have intervened from time to time in the natural evolutionary processes to nudge them forward in the right direction. As one who believes that God has on occasions performed miracles in the course of the last three or four thousand years, I see no reason to rule out this possibility. But the very length of time the evolutionary processes have taken suggests that, if there have been divine interventions, they will not have been such as to engineer any sudden 'leaps forward' or 'short cuts'.

Why should God have chosen to create us through processes of evolutionary development, rather than simply to create us from the outset as the perfectly loving and lovable souls we believe he wishes us to become? The answer, or an important part of the answer, surely is that the kind of perfection he wishes us to possess could never simply have been created by him.

This last statement may at first sight appear to be inconsistent with our belief that God is omnipotent. Could not an all-powerful God create whatever he wants to create whenever he wants to do so? The answer to this has to be that even God could not create something that is an inherent impossibility. To take a simple example, he could not make a square triangle!

It would be inherently impossible for God to have created in an instant the kind of perfection he wishes us to attain. This is because, by its very nature, the kind of perfection God wishes us to attain has to be *achieved*, through *experience*, by *each of us*. It could never simply be created by God.

God has given us freedom of will. We have to learn, from *experience*, to use our freedom wisely and well. Thus we have to learn, from experience (although we can be helped by the teaching and example of others) not to use our freedom in ways that are hurtful and harmful to other people and creatures, but to use it in ways that are lovingly helpful to them. Experience and learning are essential to what God wishes us to become. The kind of character that he wishes us ultimately to possess could not simply be created by him; it has to be created by ourselves, through the experiences and activities of living.

Central to the 'problem' of our creation as God wishes us to be is our freedom of will, and all that this entails.

It is clearly an essential part of God's plan for us that we should possess freedom of will. The highest forms of being necessarily involve the possession of freedom or self-direction – the ability, with the aid of reason, to choose between alternative courses of action, or between doing something and not doing it. Without this freedom, living creatures would either have to be governed entirely by instincts, or they would have to be controlled, like puppets or robots, by some superior being. Without freedom there could be no real personal responsibility for any kind of action, behaviour or attitude: there could be no 'achievements' or failures; there could be no moral goodness or badness; there could be no room for praise or blame, for admiration or contempt, for affection or dislike.

Without freedom there could be no real love – at least, not the highest forms of love, which embrace not just how we feel for one another, but also how we behave towards one another and what we do for one another. Such love has to be voluntarily given: it cannot be forced or automatic; and when such love is given to us, we respond to it in the way that we do because we instinctively realise that it does not have to be given. Furthermore, to be fully loving there is much that we have to learn – for example about the needs and feelings of others. An understanding love has to be developed, and developed progressively.

Of course, the exercise of freedom requires an ability to think rationally. Simple choices apart, freedom can only be used wisely when we are able to think well, and to make reasoned decisions between alternative possible actions. Likewise, to make moral choices, we need to be able to anticipate intelligently the probable consequences of our actions. In brief, freedom needs to be accompanied by brainpower. That of course is something we are born with (although we still have to learn to use it).

Besides our brains, we are born with highly complex bodies that possess all the different attributes necessary for living in our present world. These attributes – which include our various senses, our capacities for emotional and instinctive responses, and our many bodily parts that function more or less automatically – are all ones we inherit from our forebears; and they have ultimately been created through long processes of evolution. Our freedom itself, necessarily linked with brain capacity, appears to have been an evolutionary development.

Just why God has chosen to use the evolutionary methods he evidently has used to create us as we presently are is a question on which there is no need to speculate here. Suffice it that progressive evolution is the method of our creation that he has used.

As a result of our past evolution, we are born with the potential to become loving human beings in the fullest sense. What remains is for us each to achieve our potential. That is something we have to do for ourselves. Though others can guide and help us in various different ways, neither God nor anyone else could entirely do it for us.

There are doubtless other aspects to what God wishes us to become, beyond those on which I have concentrated here. Some of these too may be inherently incapable of immediate creation, but require learning and experience. For example, a sense of aesthetic appreciation surely has to be developed progressively: could we ever fully appreciate things that are beautiful without also having experienced things that are less than beautiful? Likewise, to appreciate the full wonder of God's creation we need to have a well-developed understanding of it; and a developed understanding is something else that is incapable of immediate creation, but has to be acquired. Moreover, could we ever experience the fullness of joy, if we had never experienced its absence?

Our present life, and the coming of Jesus Christ, in the context of God's plan

Seen in the context of God's whole creative plan, our life on earth must be the vital first stage of his plan for us. The world we now inhabit provides a kind of nursery for the development of our infant souls. The things that happen to us, the situations with which we are faced, the opportunities that are open to us – all these together must provide the environment in which our souls can grow, from their birth, as far as possible towards their full maturity and eventual perfection. Our experiences both good and bad, our accomplishments and achievements, and our mistakes and failures too, must provide an essential part of our souls' maturation.

So long as we are living our present lives, the best road of maturation we can follow, the way that God must wish us to follow, is surely the Christian way of life, revealed to us by Jesus Christ.

The coming of Jesus Christ has manifestly been an event of singular importance for our present life on earth. Essentially, it is clear, Jesus Christ came into the world to show us how God wishes us to live our lives – to show us what our human natures are meant to become. He came also to show us something of the true nature of God himself, and especially to show us the full extent of God's love for us.

A central part of what Jesus has done has been to give us a true sense of direction and purpose in our lives – a sense of direction and purpose that the human race was previously more or less lacking. At the same time he has 'opened up' for us the way that we should be following. The practical effect of all that he has done, for those who acknowledge him, is to make it not too difficult for us to escape from whatever may be the bonds of our past life, to join the right way, and to move forward along it.

As for the second coming of Jesus Christ, the great event that is yet to happen, the Christian Church has always believed that it will in some way mark the end of our present era of life – and, it could well be, the end of life (or at least of human life) in our world in its present form. I see no reason to think that this long-held belief is mistaken. I do not believe that God can intend our present very imperfect form of life to continue for ever.

It would be futile to speculate on just what will happen when the day comes. The prophetic words of Jesus about the things that will happen recorded in the Gospels *(Matthew 24, Mark 13, Luke 17 and 21)* should probably not all be understood too literally. Nor can we know in advance when it will be; anyone who claims to know the date, as some have, should not be taken seriously. The day could now be relatively near, not in some distant future century. But we cannot know; and we have to live both as though it could be this very day, which some day it will be, and also – for example in our care for the world's resources and environment – as though it may not be for many centuries.

What happens to souls that have not reached their intended destination in heaven?

Although the perfection of our souls must be the ultimate end of God's purpose for human beings, relatively few souls seem likely to have come near to achieving this goal by the end of our present lives. Those who have led the most saintly Christian lives may be very close to achieving it. Others who have led largely good and kind-hearted lives may not have a great deal further to go. But what about the many souls that have not come anywhere near to achieving perfection?

God's creative plan must surely allow for the limitations of our present life, and for the great differences of opportunity that it has offered, for our souls to become as he must ultimately wish. There must, I believe, be new opportunities in the next life for souls that have not yet been able to reach their final destination in heaven. In traditional terms there must be some kind of 'purgatory', during which it will be possible for the eventual perfection of our souls to be accomplished.

Inevitably, in the next life, those souls that have had little or no opportunity in this life to grow as we believe God wishes us to grow (the souls of our early ancestors almost certainly among them) will start a long way from their final destination, in terms of their eventually intended maturity and perfection. But it could be that, helped by souls that are ahead of them, they will be enabled to 'catch up' relatively quickly with souls that have advanced the furthest.

But will every soul have 'another chance' in the next life? What about those who have led the most evil kinds of life?

We cannot know of course; but it could well be that there is no group of souls so markedly worse than all others that they will be treated by God in a wholly different way from all the rest, and will be given no opportunity in the next life to redeem themselves. If, as Christians know to be true, God in this life is always ready to forgive those who repent, however bad their lives have been, why should it not be so in the next life?

We should not overlook that the most 'evil' men and women very often seem to be those who have themselves suffered harsh experiences, and who have known no real love, in their childhood. If a child is virtually rejected by its parents, if it never knows what it is to receive normal love, affection and care, if – quite possibly also – it is treated with frequent cruelty, how much can the man or woman that child becomes really be to blame for the appalling behaviour that ultimately results from his or her appalling early experiences? In the next life, the souls of such people could be unable to avoid the immediate consequences of being as they are. But they may still in time become open to receiving the love, and the help to change, that they may never have received before.

This is not to say that evil men and women may have no personal responsibility for their own actions or moral state. It is rather to say that, sometimes at least, their real culpability may not be as great in God's eyes as we are apt to judge ourselves.

As Christians have always believed, the most evil and seriously errant souls will surely find themselves, after death, in some kind of 'hell'. But in due course of time God may offer every soul some way of escape – a way by which souls that choose to do so will be able to join the road that he wishes to see them follow.

As to whether every errant soul will in the end choose to join the right road, and what might be the eventual fate of any that are unwilling to do so, it seems fruitless to speculate.

How much does it matter whether or not we live as Christians in this life?

In the light of what I have just been saying, the question is bound to arise: if it is true that every soul will in some way have another chance in the next life, how much does it matter whether in this life we live as Christians, or remain either unbelievers or followers of some other faith?

The traditional Christian belief has been that only those who accept and follow the Christian faith can be judged worthy of salvation, and will in due course find a place in heaven. This belief is primarily based on what Jesus himself is recorded as having said, notably:

> I am the way and the truth and the life. No-one comes to the Father except through me. *(John 14.6, NIV)*

And there are other statements to similar effect in the New Testament, for example:

> Salvation is found in no-one else [but Jesus Christ], for there is no other name under heaven given to men by which we must be saved. *(Acts 4.12, NIV)*

Especially on account of these texts, there are probably many Christians today who still uphold the traditional belief that only those who are followers of Jesus Christ can achieve salvation. But those who like myself cannot accept the traditional beliefs about judgement, heaven and hell, entailing a final and irreversible judgement for every person at the end of our present lives, naturally tend also to reject the traditional view about what will happen in the next life to those who are non-Christians. The texts I have just quoted, like others on the subject of judgement, should not be interpreted as being true in their most literal sense; for the implications of doing so could surely *not* be true. The souls of those who in this life remain unbelievers or followers of other faiths could surely not on that account, regardless of the quality of their lives, be permanently debarred from finding a place in heaven.

But that does not mean that it little matters whether or not we live as Christians in this life. If, as all Christians believe, Christian beliefs are the true (or truest) beliefs – or, as some might prefer to say, are true to a greater extent than the beliefs of any other religion – and if the

Christian way of life is without doubt the surest and best road that we can follow (it must be in some such sense that we should interpret the texts just quoted), then it must be that the sooner we join this road the better.

Other roads can lead in all kinds of different directions, but some of them may take us in more or less the direction that we need to go. How far they take us will depend, as indeed for Christian believers too, on the general quality of our lives. The lives of unbelievers can be influenced by Christian values; and of course other faiths, to some extent at least, proclaim similar values. What is always missing for unbelievers is any relationship with God. Sometimes quite possibly, and especially for devout followers of other faiths, another road may lead a long way in more or less the right direction. But the Christian road still remains by far the surest road to follow, and it is the road that looks to go furthest in the right direction. This being so, Christians can continue to see it as the one wholly true road of life.

Chapter 16

Why must there be so much Pain and Suffering in this Life?

OUR present life is overshadowed by pain and suffering. Whether or not we ourselves are presently suffering under some form of affliction, no person of humanity can fail to be affected and distressed by the sufferings of so many people in the world around us. Indeed, the more we mature as human beings, the more we become alive to the sufferings of others. In the world in which we live, none of us can escape from suffering.

Of course, there is also much in life that is good. Though there are tragically many people in our world for whom life is continuously hard, for the majority of us in the Western world today our lives are far from being always dominated by pain and suffering. Although there are times when we cannot escape them, there is much in life that we are able to enjoy. God surely means us to enjoy the good things of life when we reasonably and rightly can. But what about pain and suffering?

How can a God of love be responsible for creating a world in which there is so much suffering? How could a God of justice be responsible for a world in which there is so much unjust, undeserved, suffering? Could there have been no better way for God to achieve his ultimate purpose, without all the pain and suffering of this world?

In the present chapter I will be seeking to address these difficult questions, and suggesting some possible answers, or the beginnings of some possible answers, to them.

Possible explanations for the existence of pain and suffering
At the most fundamental level, there are a number of different ways in which people may seek to explain the existence of pain and suffering. The outlines of four such ways are summarised below.

- *Atheist explanations.* The existence of our universe, and of life on our own planet, is essentially an accident, and so is the form that life has taken. Once the big bang had happened, as scientists now understand (or have begun to understand, for their understanding is yet far from complete), everything followed a natural course of its own accord, though with chance events playing a major part in the outcome. Life on earth, and in due course the development of pain and suffering, emerged through a combination of chance events and the natural processes of evolution. So also did death, as the natural termination of life for individual creatures.
- *A possible theist explanation.* Contrary to the conviction of atheists, there is a God who originally created our universe. However, he is not by any means the God of infinite wisdom and love in whom Christians and also Jews and Muslims believe, and he has created a very imperfect world, in which we find ourselves. Pain and suffering, which have emerged through the natural processes of evolution, are the result of an imperfect world created by an imperfect God.
- *The traditional Christian belief.* God originally made everything in our world as he intended it to be. However, his intentions were corrupted through the work of the devil. Pain, suffering and death are the result of our human fall from grace, following the first sin of Adam and Eve.
- *A modern Christian explanation.* Our universe and world, and life in our world, have evolved in accordance with God's purpose and plan. The existence of pain and suffering does not destroy our conviction that God is a God of infinite wisdom and love – a love that we see demonstrated especially through the life, death and resurrection of Jesus Christ. However difficult we may find it to understand the reasons, the pain and suffering of our present world appear to be unavoidable features of God's creative plan – a plan that will be fulfilled in a future life that is yet to come.

The first of these explanations does I think broadly sum up what thinking atheists believe, although they might put it in different terms.

As to the second explanation – that our universe is the creation of an imperfect God – this seems a reasonable viewpoint for anyone who is inclined to believe that there must be a God, but who has difficulty in believing that he really can be a God of love, because of the existence of pain and suffering. If any of you reading this book have been thinking along these lines, I hope in this chapter to persuade you that it is possible to reconcile the existence of pain and suffering with Christian belief in a God of perfect wisdom and love.

The third explanation – that pain and suffering came into the world as a result of the corruption of God's creation that started when Adam and Eve fell into sin in response to temptation by the devil – summarises what most if not all Christians believed until around the second half of the nineteenth century. There are probably still many Christians worldwide who continue to hold beliefs along these lines.

There may well be many other Christians today who do not see the fall of Adam and Eve as an historical event, but who believe that the devil must have a high responsibility, or at least a partial responsibility, for the pain and suffering of our world and all its evils. This alternative belief requires some comment.

Christians today differ on the question of whether or not the devil really exists – a subject discussed in an annexe to this chapter. Almost certainly the majority of Christians do believe in the devil's existence; but among liberally inclined theologians (both conservative and radical) there are a good many who either have doubts or are outright disbelievers.

Assuming the devil does exist his main role, as Christians have generally believed it to be, is that of tempting or prompting human beings to behave in ways that are contrary to the will of God. For those who accept our evolutionary origins, the devil could hardly have a direct responsibility for the *existence* of pain and suffering, which appear to be essential features of life as it has evolved, and must have come into existence long before there were human beings. But the devil can be presumed to have a substantial responsibility for the worst forms of human behaviour, which can cause great suffering to others. He must then have a responsibility for the *extent* of human suffering.

To those who doubt the devil's existence, on the other hand, all forms of antisocial behaviour that cause suffering to others appear capable of being explained in purely human terms. It is an inevitable consequence of our freedom that people will often use that freedom in ways that are hurtful and harmful to others. We are all naturally inclined to be selfish and self-centred. Although, accidents apart, we quickly learn to avoid doing things that will obviously cause hurt to ourselves, we are much slower at learning to avoid acting in ways that cause others to suffer. To behave with consideration for others is not innate in us; it is something that we each of us have to learn. Largely or partly through differences in upbringing different people learn it in different degrees. There are some who never learn it, and become prone to behaving in highly antisocial ways. People who behave in the worst and most grossly antisocial ways, with no apparent concern for how others are affected, are commonly described as psychopaths, and psychologists are able to give reasonably convincing explanations of their behaviour without bringing in any supernatural diabolical influence.

In brief, for those who doubt the devil's existence, even the very worst forms of human behaviour, both individual and collective, appear to be fully explainable in human terms. The evils of our world that are linked with human actions, and the suffering that results, are the responsibility of human beings alone.

In the rest of this chapter I will be giving a 'modern' Christian explanation of why there has to be pain and suffering in our world. The influence of the devil will not be mentioned as a possible contributory factor. However, readers who believe that he must have played a part are free to extend the explanations I suggest, where this seems appropriate.

Before proceeding, I should make it clear that although I think we can see the answers, or partial answers, to some of the questions we will be addressing, there will also be questions that cannot be answered with any certainty. To know the full answers we would need to have a far more complete understanding of God's creative plan than we can yet have.

Pain and suffering can take a considerable number of different forms, both physical and mental, and to some extent different considerations can apply to different forms of them. Here, however, I will be seeking to deal only with certain specific issues, and some simplification should be in order. The particular subjects we will be considering are as follows:

- First, some of the main useful functions of pain and suffering.
- Second, suffering that appears to serve no good purpose. Under this heading there are two related questions:
  - Could not God have stopped people from causing great suffering to others?
  - Why does God allow our natural world to result in so much suffering?
- Third, could not God have found a better way of achieving his purpose, without all the pain and suffering of our present world?
- Fourth, can the creator of our unjustly suffering world really be a God of infinite wisdom and love?

Some functions of pain and suffering

It is clear that the primary biological function of pain, and of other forms of suffering such as hunger and thirst, is to serve as nature's way of guiding our behaviour. As such, pain and suffering are all-important for the survival of every form of animal life in which behaviour is not entirely automatic or instinctive. Hunger and thirst tell us that we need to eat and drink, tiredness that we need to sleep. Pain, which is typically the consequence of some damage to our own bodies, is nature's way of telling us that we need to protect our bodies from harm. If there were no pain, living creatures that are free to control their own actions would surely become careless of their bodies, and thus careless of their lives. A tragic example is people with severe leprosy, who ultimately lose their fingers because they have ceased to feel pain in them.

What we call the 'survival' instinct is essentially the natural instinct to avoid pain and suffering.

Though we do not know for certain, the likelihood is that pain and suffering will have originated around the time that relatively primitive living creatures started to develop a degree of control over their own movements or actions, and parts of their behaviour ceased to be entirely automatic or instinctive. From that time on, unpleasant feelings will have been needed to help guide their behaviour and improve their prospects of survival.

Pain and suffering must also have played an important part in the later stages of animal evolution. For it must typically have been the impulse to avoid suffering (whether in the form of injury, starvation, thirst or exposure to cold) that caused groups of creatures to respond to changing circumstances by changing their habits, so as to improve their prospects of survival. This in turn will sometimes have led, in course of time, to evolutionary changes in their physical characteristics.

Apart from the main biological functions of pain to which I have just referred, it is apparent that pain and suffering can serve some other ultimately beneficial purposes. Notably, there are a various ways in which they can help to promote the development of our personalities along the lines that God must intend.

Though it is not always so, we can be helped to mature through personal suffering. The experience of suffering – whether it be a serious illness, an unpleasant accident, a period of real anxiety, or a close family bereavement – can cause us to think and feel in ways in which we have not thought or felt before, and can make us conscious of realities and truths that are new to us. Through suffering, our tendencies to complacency and self-satisfaction are lessened. Then the support and sympathy we receive from others can help us to become more appreciative of other people than we were before. Moreover, through our own suffering we can gain a better insight into the sufferings of others, and so can ourselves become more sensitive and sympathetic to the feelings of others.

In such ways, it seems that suffering can help to broaden our outlook, to deepen our understanding, to soften the hard edges of our character, and to create in us a somehow more rounded personality.

Then again, the sight of other people's suffering can arouse the altruistic side of our natures, and encourage its development, in ways that would perhaps otherwise not be possible. So, through our practical response to the sufferings of others, we become more caring and more kind-hearted – we become, in fact, more fully human. Indeed, in a world in which everyone was 'all right', could we ever learn to become truly caring for one another?

More generally, when living creatures find life easy and pleasurable, with nothing to disturb their enjoyment, they commonly have no desire for change – unless it be for something even more easy and pleasurable! It is only when life starts to become difficult or unpleasant that we begin to contemplate the need to alter our ways or our situation. And it seems clear that this common feature of life in our present world – the tendency to make changes primarily in order to avoid pain, suffering or unpleasantness – must always have been a crucial one in the long processes, first, of animal evolution, and then of human social development.

Suffering that appears to serve no good purpose

To recognise the beneficial consequences that can flow from the existence of pain and suffering is not to argue that, in every instance of actual suffering, the outcome will always in some sense be favourable. All too often, the reverse seems clearly to be so. For example sometimes, quite apart from its direct unpleasantness, suffering can make people embittered, resentful or revengeful: their personalities, instead of being matured by it, seem to become warped by it. Others seem to be defeated, and diminished, by prolonged adversity. And sometimes the extremity of suffering, whether for a single person or for a group of people, is so great that it can look almost impossible to conceive that any longer-term 'good' that may result could outweigh the immediate 'bad'.

Moreover the benefits of suffering could hardly be said to be fairly apportioned. For though it can be said that there are a great many people whose personalities have been helped to mature as a result of suffering – whether through their own suffering or through their responses to the sufferings of others – there are a great many others who appear to be far more its victims than its beneficiaries.

So, though we may see the general necessity for the existence of pain and suffering, we may still feel inclined to ask: could not God at least have prevented the very worst cases of suffering, where the consequences are almost wholly bad?

The sufferings of our world appear to stem, mostly at least, from two main kinds of immediate cause. The one is wrongful human actions, whether deliberate or careless or merely ignorant (or human inaction where action is needed). The other is through mal-effects arising from the normal workings of our natural world – under which heading come natural disasters such as earthquakes, floods, droughts and violent storms, and also bodily diseases. So the question of whether God could not have prevented the worst cases of suffering, where the consequences are almost wholly bad, really breaks down into two separate questions:

- Could not God have intervened to prevent us using our freedom in ways that cause great suffering to others?
- Why does God allow our natural world to result in so much suffering?

Could not God have stopped people from causing great suffering to others?

God has given us freedom of will, and it is quite difficult to imagine by just what means he might have controlled our worst behaviour, if he had wished to do so. But leaving that question aside, it is evident that if he had chosen in some way to stop people acting in ways that cause substantial suffering to others, his control would need to be extensive to make a significant difference to the sum of human suffering. There are so many kinds of human action that, directly or indirectly, cause considerable suffering to others. If, hypothetically, God did choose to exercise a certain degree of control over our actions, the question would constantly be arising: why did he not stop him or her doing that? Indeed, from God's point of view, how could he draw a line between when to intervene and when not to do so?

These difficulties apart, if God did somehow superimpose a method of control over our behaviour that effectively removed a substantial amount of our freedom, could we ever learn to become fully responsible for our own actions? Could we ever learn to use our freedom wisely and well? If God always prevented our worst actions could we ever learn to become mature, thoughtful, responsible and caring people?

I do not think it could really have made sense for God to limit the freedom he has given us.

Why does God allow our natural world to result in so much suffering?

Why does our natural world result in so many disasters, such as earthquakes, hurricanes, droughts and floods? Why are we so much afflicted by illness and disease? Why are children born with physical or mental disabilities?

Scientists seek to answer questions of this kind by finding out the causes of the problems they are investigating. At present, there are still many such questions they cannot answer, or can only partly answer; but in principle, they are probably all capable of being given full scientific explanations. For example, quite a lot is now known about how earthquakes happen, and similarly with extreme weather conditions. We have also started to have some understanding of the origins of diseases and genetic defects. There still remains much that is not known, but it seems clear that what we think of as disorders of our natural world are ultimately nothing more nor less than the outcome of the ways in which our natural world has evolved.

Answers along these lines may be enough for those who have no belief in God. But for those of us who see God as the creator of our universe, and believe him to be a God of infinite wisdom and love, they are not sufficient answers. (Nor will they be enough for those who are open to believing in God, but have doubts because of the pain and suffering of our world.) We would like to know why God has designed the world as it is, or at least has allowed it to evolve as it has. Could he not somehow have prevented the disorders of our natural world?

No one can really know the answers to these most fundamental questions about why our natural world works as it does, and so often appears to work badly. But I think there are two main possible kinds of answer (apart from answers that may be given by those who have no belief in a loving God). These are:

- What we see as malfunctions of our natural world are unavoidable features of the creative plan that God has chosen (much as the existence of pain, and of physical death, appear to be inherent features of his chosen plan). Moreover, sometimes at least, the apparent malfunctions may serve some important purposes, which are not immediately apparent to us.
- What we see as malfunctions of our natural world are in the nature of 'design defects' in it, which with the benefit of hindsight God could have overcome by making some modifications to his original 'design plan' for our world.

The second possible answer, that God originally made certain 'mistakes' in his design of our physical world, has never been a Christian view. It would imply that, contrary to what Christians generally believe, God is not a God of infinite wisdom. I think it unlikely that the natural disasters, illnesses and diseases that are a common feature of our world could have been, for God, unforeseen consequences of his creation. The first answer seems much more likely to be the correct one.

Thus, as regards natural disasters, the world we inhabit today is the product of progressive change over billions of years. Our physical world has never been altogether stable. That applies equally to the surface of the earth, to what lies below the surface, and to the climatic conditions of the world. What we think of as natural disasters could be unavoidable features of a world that must in some degree continue to undergo physical change.

Something of the same may well apply to genetic defects. These too may be unavoidable features of a living order in which genetic variations can take place. (And genetic variations appear to have played an essential part in the processes of evolution.) It could well be impossible to have a genetic system that is capable of producing good and useful variations, but could never produce bad ones.

Illnesses and diseases could also be unavoidable features of evolving physical life. That aside, it could be said that they can serve a number of ultimately useful purposes in helping us to develop socially in the kinds of ways that God must wish. We learn from their existence that we must endeavour to look after ourselves properly: for healthy survival, life can never be a matter of 'anything goes'. Of course we have first to learn to understand the things that can cause illnesses and diseases; and as with everything else about our world we are bound to start from ignorance. But the processes of increasing our knowledge and understanding of our world appear themselves to be an important part of human maturation.

Besides this, a significant part of our more recent social development has been linked with endeavouring to overcome disease, and with all that we do to care for those who are afflicted by illness and disease.

It may still be asked, could not God intervene to stop natural events of a kind that may have served some useful purposes in the past, but today merely cause suffering?

As with the question of possible divine interventions to prevent human beings from acting in ways that cause considerable suffering to others, it is difficult to visualise just what form or forms God's intervention to stop natural events might hypothetically take. There is also the question of the extent to which the supernatural prevention of natural events might have harmful side effects, or create further problems for the future. Leaving these issues aside, however, it is clear that God's interventions would again need to be on a substantial scale to make a material difference to the amount of suffering that arises from the many different apparent malfunctionings of nature.

God has chosen to create a physical world that is governed by what we call laws of nature ('laws' of which we now have a considerable, though not yet complete, understanding). I do not think it could then really make sense for him to make a frequent practice of interfering with the normal workings of nature. Were he to do so, apart from any other consequences, our natural world would certainly become an unpredictable environment in which to live.

(While it appears that God has on occasions acted in such a way as to override the normal laws of nature by performing what we call miracles, these interventions are so exceptional that for practical purposes they do not undermine the general order and predictability of our natural world.)

Let us sum up the arguments so far. In our world as it is, pain and suffering serve a number of useful purposes. Quite often, in particular cases they serve no good purpose that we can see. But useful purpose or no, God could not have prevented the suffering that results from the misuse of human freedom, other than by (somehow) substantially curtailing our freedom. Nor, probably, could he have prevented the suffering that arises from what we see as disorders of our natural world. Whether or not these 'disorders' now serve any useful purpose, they could well be unavoidable features of our world as God has intentionally created it. In any event, were he in some way to intervene to stop them from happening, his interventions would need to be very frequent to make much difference to the total of human suffering, which itself would make our physical world an unpredictable place in which to live.

The conclusion that pain and suffering, in all the different forms that we know, appear to be unavoidable features of our world as God has chosen to create it leads to a further question that now needs to be addressed. Could not God have found a better way of achieving his purpose, without all the pain and suffering of our present world?

Could not God have found a better way of achieving his purpose?

It is clearly not possible to give a direct answer to the question posed. We simply cannot know whether or not there were other possible ways by which God could have set out to achieve his purpose, besides the way he has actually chosen. But as most Christians will see it, if there had been a better way, without any pain and suffering, or without as much pain and suffering as there is in our present world, then God would have chosen it. That belief stems from our conviction that he really is a God of infinite wisdom and love.

It is a characteristic of Christians generally that, in spite of all the difficulties in understanding why there has to be so much pain and suffering in this present world, we still believe that God is a God of infinite wisdom, love and justice. The fact of pain and suffering has not destroyed this belief. How we are able to reconcile our belief about God's nature with the fact of pain and suffering is the subject of the next and final main section of this chapter.

Reverting to our present question, it seems to me that in any kind of world in which living creatures with freedom of will are meant by God to learn from experience to look after themselves, and also to use their freedom in such a way as to behave with caring love towards other creatures, there could be a practical necessity for 'wrong' forms of behaviour to have some kind of unpleasant consequences. Moreover, if creatures with freedom are ever to learn to act with caring love for others, suffering will often need to fall *undeservedly* (as it does in our present world). For if suffering fell only on those who deserved to suffer, in proportion to their deserts, would we ever think it necessary, or right, to do anything to relieve it? Could we ever learn to act with caring, unselfish love, in a world in which there was no undeserved suffering?

I think the answers to these last questions probably has to be no. But it would be altogether beyond me to demonstrate that there was in fact no better way that God could have chosen than the way he has! In the end that can only be a matter for our faith in him.

Can the creator of our unjustly suffering world really be a God of infinite wisdom, love and justice?

It is an observable fact that most of the sufferings of our world fall on people who appear to be innocent, or relatively so, and who could hardly be said to deserve what they suffer.

The victims of earthquakes, floods, droughts or other natural disasters; most of the victims of war and of terrorism; the more or less powerless victims of corrupt and oppressive governments; the victims of religious or racial persecution; the victims of many forms of criminal activity; the victims of judicial injustice, convicted of crimes they did not commit; victims of tragic accidents; the victims of disabling illnesses; the victims of particularly painful or unpleasant illnesses; children born with severe disabilities and their families; young children who are the victims of cruel parents; most of the victims of prolonged unemployment and poverty . . . : in all such cases we see people suffering to a far greater extent than they could be said to 'deserve'.

Jesus Christ himself was the wholly innocent victim of deliberate gross judicial injustice.

On the other hand, those who carry the greatest responsibility for causing others to suffer often do not appear, in this present life, to suffer very much themselves – or certainly not in proportion to the suffering they have caused others.

There is no sign of justice in the way that the sufferings of our present world are distributed. Sometimes, it is true, people's wrongful actions do sooner or later cause their own suffering in one way or another. But much of our world's suffering is simply a matter of chance. In the distant past (as a good many passages in the Old Testament bear witness) it was thought that God somehow controlled the incidence of suffering according to what people deserved; but in reality how it falls is largely accidental. It falls on whom it happens to fall, regardless of deserts.

God does not control who suffers. But he is, in a very real sense, ultimately responsible for all the sufferings of our world. For while it is true that much of the immediate responsibility rests with human beings, it was God who chose to make the world as it is, and who has allowed us to develop freedom of will. He must therefore have a responsibility for our inevitable frequent failures to use our freedom wisely and well. He must also have responsibility for the workings of our natural world, and for the suffering that results from these.

How can we reconcile the evident fact of God's ultimate responsibility for suffering, and much of it in practice undeserved suffering, with our conviction that he is a God of infinite wisdom, love and justice?

I do not think it would be possible to base any reconciliation on the view that all that is good in our present life (and of course there is much that is good!) is sufficient to outweigh all the pain and suffering of it. This may be more or less true for many people living in the more prosperous and better governed countries of the world today; but there are, and probably always have been, so many others for whom it has clearly not been true. Even if, numerically, there are more people whose lives have been mostly enjoyable than people whose lives have been predominantly the reverse, there could be no justice in setting off one group against the other!

If this world were all that there is, and this life were all that there is, it would simply not be possible to reconcile the fact of pain and suffering, so much of it undeserved, with our conviction that God is a God of infinite wisdom, love and justice. But as Christians, we are convinced that this life we know now is not all that there is. Our present life with all its suffering and injustice is no more than a kind of preliminary training for the 'main' life, which will follow death. So we are able to believe (and do believe) that the sufferings of this life are a price that has to be paid – and a price that must be worth paying – for all the splendour of the life that is to come. We can also believe that, in some way we cannot now expect to know, there will be some compensation provided by God for the 'unfair' sufferings of this life, which in differing degrees are borne by so many people.

Much as human parents suffer anguish when their children suffer, God himself must surely in some way share in all our sufferings. Just what he must himself suffer, to know all the appalling things that happen day after day throughout our world, lies beyond our imagination. What we can rather imagine is that there must be many times every day when he would really like to act in order to stop what is happening! Yet he must always be constrained from doing so. For were he to make a practice of intervening in the affairs of our world – were he in some way to remove, override or limit our freedom to act as we choose – it would surely in effect mean aborting his whole creative plan and purpose. He can therefore have no real choice but to wait for us to learn to act ourselves as he must long to see us do.

It must also be that he can allow, and share in, all the sufferings of our world only because he himself knows them to be the unavoidable price of the far greater good that will ultimately be achieved.

This indeed has always been the Christian conviction – a conviction that can be summed up in the words of St Paul, who himself had often experienced the full reality of suffering:

> I consider that what we suffer at this present time cannot be compared at all with the glory that is going to be revealed to us. *(Romans 8.18, GNB)*

Concluding comments

At the start of this chapter, I set out four different possible lines of explanation for the existence of pain and suffering. These were:

- that there is no God, and that pain and suffering are part of the 'accident' of creation;
- that pain and suffering are the result of an imperfect world, created by an imperfect God;
- that our world was originally made as God intended it to be, without pain and suffering, and without death, but it was corrupted through the work of the devil;
- that the pain and suffering of our present world appear to be unavoidable features of God's creative plan, the fulfilment of which lies in a future life that is yet to come.

In the end, if we are looking for an ultimate explanation of why there is pain and suffering in our present world, we have to decide which of these lines of explanation (or perhaps some other one) appears most likely to be the true one. It will be clear that we cannot come to a personal view in isolation from our beliefs about the existence and nature of God himself, and about the likely nature of his plan in creation.

Certainly, we can only reconcile the fact of pain and suffering, so much of it undeserved, with the Christian conviction that God is a God of infinite wisdom, love and justice, if we also believe (as Christians do) that his ultimate purpose and plan for us lie beyond our present world.

The world in which we live is a very imperfect one. But it must be good for the purposes for which God intends it. In it, we can see and experience both what is good and what is evil. To discover and achieve perfection, we have to experience imperfection, as well as to know what is good.

In the journey of our present life, in which we come to know and experience both good and evil, we are meant to discover something of the vision of God, the vision of all that is perfect. In the eventual history of God's creation, our journey has only just begun. In the end, all that is evil will be left behind, and only the good will remain.

Annexe to Chapter 16

Does the Devil Exist?

MY purpose in what follows is not to argue for any particular conclusion about the devil's existence, but rather to explain the main reasons why Christians have different views.

For those who believe in his existence, as most Christians probably do, the devil (or Satan, as he was first called) is a personal spiritual power of evil, who is continually working to defeat the good purposes of God. An alternative version of the belief is that he is the chief of an organised multitude of lesser demons. He has the power to influence human actions for the worse, either by feeding evil thoughts and temptations into our minds, or by reinforcing evil inclinations we already have. In many views, also, it is possible for human beings to become so 'possessed' by the devil that he is virtually in full control of their behaviour.

Belief in the existence and activities of the devil was more or less universal within the Christian Church until around the middle of the nineteenth century. However, in more recent years, along with the doctrine of the historical fall of man through the first sin of Adam and Eve in response to the devil's temptation, the existence of the devil has become quite widely questioned, particularly among liberally inclined theologians in the Western world. (Among Christians generally, the belief has almost certainly not become as widely questioned as the historical fall itself.)

The origins of belief in the devil are uncertain. In the Old Testament there are only a small number of references to him, and he is there referred to entirely as Satan. In the well-known story of Adam and Eve in the book of Genesis, it was a serpent who tempted them to eat the forbidden fruit *(Genesis 3.1–13)*, and it was only later that the serpent came to be seen as the personification of the devil. Outside Judaism there were certainly pagan societies that believed in the existence of evil spirits, and it could be that the Jewish belief in Satan as the chief of evil spirits was influenced by earlier pagan beliefs.

In due course it became the Jewish, and subsequently Christian, belief that Satan was originally the leader of a group of rebellious angels, who were banished from heaven by God. Though this belief is not found in the Old Testament, there are some references to it in the New Testament *(2 Peter 2.4; Jude verse 6; Revelation 12.7–9)*. The earliest surviving accounts of it are in non-biblical Jewish literature of the second century BC.

In the New Testament there are a good many references to the activities of the devil, and it is clear that by the time of Jesus he was seen as responsible not only for evil temptations and behaviour, but also for various forms of illness and disability, both physical and mental. In the Gospels, Jesus is quite often recorded as mentioning the devil, Satan, Beelzebub or the Evil One (which were other names for him).

From the very beginning, the Christian Church accepted without question the prevailing beliefs about the devil. Over the following centuries, belief in his existence remained generally undoubted until the nineteenth century.

There are I think three main reasons why over the past century or more, the existence of the devil has come to be doubted by a fair number, if still only a minority, of Christians. These are:

- Except among creationists, it is no longer believed to be an historical fact that Adam and Eve were created by God as the first man and woman, and lived in accordance with his will until they fell to the temptation of the devil, this being the origin of all human evil. The existence of human evil can now, in principle, be fully explained in human terms, in the light of our evolutionary origins, without bringing in the influence of some supernatural power of evil. In effect, human wrongdoing in all its forms can be seen as an inevitable consequence of our freedom.
- In origin, Jewish belief in the devil appears more likely than not to have been an invention of human minds, influenced by already existing pagan beliefs, to try to account for why there was so much evil in a world created by a God who is wholly good.
- There is seen to be no convincing independent evidence of the devil's existence.

None of these arguments is conclusive, and various counter-arguments can be made. Thus, though the Genesis story of the origin of evil can now be seen as unhistorical, that is not to say that the devil does not exist. Similarly, even if it was human thinking, unaided by any divine inspiration, that first saw him to exist, that thinking could have hit upon the truth. And as regards evidence of the devil's existence, there have certainly been many Christians who claim to have experienced his reality – for example in the form of an unmistakable evil 'presence', in the form of an experience of being tempted by him, or in the form of people whose behaviour is seen to be the result of diabolical possession. (Others can doubt the true validity of such evidence, and see possible alternative explanations of the phenomena in question.)

For Christians who believe in the devil's existence, the Bible itself is usually seen to provide the strongest grounds for doing so. As already mentioned, in the New Testament especially there are numerous references to the devil, and Christians who believe the biblical authors to have been incapable of error naturally accept the Bible's views of the devil's existence.

For Christians who do not believe that the Bible authors were infallible, there still remains the fact that, as the Gospels record, Jesus himself quite often referred to the devil and his works. Moreover he does so in ways that, sometimes at least, give no good grounds for thinking that he was speaking in purely metaphorical terms. From what the Gospels tell us, there seems little doubt that Jesus accepted the contemporary belief in the existence and activities of the devil. There are probably many Christians who see this as providing more or less conclusive grounds for continuing to hold this belief. Surely Jesus himself could not be mistaken?

There are others who see it differently. In the view of many theologians, though Jesus must have been enlightened to an exceptional degree through the Holy Spirit, in his human life he could not have had the unlimited knowledge that God himself has. Apart from any specific knowledge that may have come to him through some special revelation, he could only have the knowledge that he was able to acquire as an exceptionally enlightened and intelligent man of his time. Thus, though we are not told, it seems likely that he will have accepted as historical the

Genesis account of the creation and fall of man. For him, as for all his contemporaries, the idea of our evolutionary origins was then of course entirely unknown. As regards the devil, without some revelation on the subject, he could not have known whether or not the generally accepted Jewish beliefs on the subject were true. It is quite possible that he could have had some private doubts about these beliefs. But if he had, he could well also have felt that there would be no virtue in expressing his doubts publicly. There was already quite enough about the practice of Jewish religion that he did need to question!

In any event, there are a fair number of Christians who do not see Jesus' references to the devil as unquestionable grounds for accepting the belief.

For myself, I see no compelling reason for being convinced that the devil does exist and some reasons for doubting his existence; but equally I am far from being certain that he does not exist.

Whether or not there exists a universal supernatural power of evil, there appears to be quite a lot of evidence of localised spiritual presences that are perceived as having an aura of evil about them. It could also sometimes be that certain people can fall under the influence of a particular evil spirit – a view that is certainly held by those who practise the Christian ministry of exorcism. To my mind, however, these kinds of phenomena do not necessarily signify the existence of an organised worldwide spiritual power of evil.

Whether the devil as a universal power of evil exists or not, we certainly live in a world in which the hearts and minds of human beings can be infected in one way or another with every known kind of evil. And whether he exists or not, we have to work as best we can, with the spiritual help that God can give us, to overcome the power of evil in all its different forms by the power of good.

Chapter 17

Why does God Hide his Presence from us?

Of the questions posed at the beginning of this section of the book on page 78, there remains one we have still to consider: why should God keep his presence hidden from us, as he does? This question I will now seek to answer; and I will follow with a second quite closely linked question: given that God hides his presence from us, how can we start moving towards our ultimate goal, as Christians believe it to be, of knowing him in all his fullness?

It is not I think too difficult to see a probable answer, or at least a partial answer, to the first of our two questions: why does God keep his presence hidden from us?

Freedom of will appears to be an essential feature of our human development, as God has planned it. But could we really be 'free', if we were conscious of God's presence? If we were fully aware of his presence, would not our whole being be totally dominated by that awareness? Would we not find ourselves literally powerless, if he really revealed to us his own infinite power? If God were to reveal just a little of himself to you, here and now, would you not be totally overwhelmed? (Indeed, by accounts, those who do have some powerful experience of the divine presence are, for the time being, overwhelmed.)

The need for us to be free from the overpowering dominance of God, at least until our souls have reached a considerable degree of maturity – and we are able, as it were, to stand up in his presence – could well be a main reason why he has chosen to hide his presence from us in this life. Only so can we have the independence necessary for our earlier development and growth.

Let us turn now to the second question: how are we to start making progress towards the eventual full knowledge of God?

It must be that we can only come to the fullest possible knowledge of God in all his reality by a number, and maybe a great number, of gradual steps. God being everything that he must be, we could hardly expect to move, more or less in an instant, from a total ignorance to a full knowledge of him!

Of necessity, we start from total ignorance of him. We generally do not even know of his existence, unless someone else tells us about him, and we believe what we are told!

Once we really believe that he does exist, then we can start to 'look for' him, and to make ourselves 'open' to him. This will tend to happen automatically as we start to follow the way of Christian life, and develop the practice of prayer, which will bring us closer to him. And sooner or later it can sometimes be that God will choose in one manner or another to reveal just enough of himself to turn a belief into certainty.

Some people may progress further, and achieve more advanced forms of 'mystical' experience of God's reality. But up till now such men and women have been relatively few; and they appear to have been drawn only from those who have wholly committed their lives to him, and who have also advanced in the kind of prayer we call 'contemplation'.

This, it seems, is the furthest that anyone can go towards directly knowing God, in our present life. All the rest must lie in the life to come.

Historically also, we can see the broad steps by which God has made it possible for us to come to our present knowledge and understanding of him. He has done this first of all, as we can deduce from the books of the Old Testament, by means of successive revelations of himself to individual men, in the course of the early history of the Jewish nation. The first such person to whom he revealed himself could well have been the man we know as Abraham, recognised as the founding father of the Jewish nation.

(The opening book of the Bible, Genesis, tells us of other people before Abraham who had knowledge of God; but many theologians think that the events and personalities described in the earlier chapters of this book probably have no historical basis, and are entirely legendary. Some, but I think only a minority, question Abraham's existence too.)

Why does God Hide his Presence from us?

Through Abraham, through the generations that immediately followed him, in due course through the great Israelite prophet and leader Moses, and later still through a succession of other prophets, our knowledge and understanding of God has been gradually extended, by means of revelations of himself to individual men.

Then at last came the time for God to take the most decisive step he has yet taken, in making more about himself known to us. He sent his own Son Jesus Christ into the world to become born as man.

As Christians have always recognised, Jesus Christ came into the world not only to show us how God means us to live our lives. He came also to lead us to a greater knowledge and love of God, to enable us to understand, much more than we ever could before, what God's nature is really like. Indeed we believe that in the person of Jesus, as we can know his nature from the four Gospels, we can see something of the true nature of God himself.

Jesus Christ has shown us that we can each of us come to know something of God personally, and to love him as our Heavenly Father, as we seek to live our lives according to his will.

* * * * *

I have now completed the principal task I set for myself in this book — that of explaining the main essentials of the Christian faith. I hope that I will have written enough to enable you, the reader, to make your own judgement about the truth, or likely truth, of the main Christian beliefs. (If you should now like a summary of what I have been saying, may I invite you to reread chapter 1.)

If you are persuaded that Christian beliefs as I have described them are true, or likely to be true, or not too far from the truth, then if you are not already a practising Christian you may wish to become one.

The four chapters of Part II are intended mainly for readers who have not been practising Christians, but who have either come to the point of wanting to become so, or at least have reached the point of starting to think about it. The first of them gives some guidance on the main initial steps that need to be taken, to set out along the road of living fully as a Christian. The following three chapters consider the subjects of prayer, reading the Bible, and the Holy Spirit in Christian life.

PART II

FOR THOSE WHO MAY WISH TO BECOME PRACTISING CHRISTIANS

Chapter 18

Becoming a Practising Christian

THERE is, or certainly can be, a substantial difference between being just a Christian believer (a person who has come to believe that the main doctrines of the Christian faith are true), and being a fully committed practising Christian. The former need involve only our intellect, whereas the latter must involve something much more: it means our Christian faith has come to be at the centre of our life, and we aspire as best we can to be true followers of Jesus Christ.

How do you actually become a practising Christian?

There is no single answer to this question. People can become committed practising Christians in different ways, by different routes. For some it can be through a more or less instantaneous experience of 'conversion': one day they were hardly Christians at all; the next day, as a result of a radical inner change of heart and mind, in which there is commonly a strong sense that God himself has played a leading part, they have become fully desirous of following the way of Christian life. At the other end of the spectrum there are those who become committed Christians through a much more gradual series of progressive steps, which extend over a period of some years. And of course there is a range of possibilities in between.

What follows is intended to offer some guidance to the person who is ready to think about becoming a practising Christian, or at least about starting to move forward in that direction. What should you do?

The first requirement for becoming a practising Christian normally is that you should, in some degree, want to do so; or at least that some part of you should want to do so, though there may be other parts of you that do not! I will return to this subject at the end of the chapter.

Assuming that you do want to do so, I would say that there are four main steps you will need to take, if you are to become a fully practising

Christian. They are steps you may either take more or less at once and all together, or take progressively over a period of time.

The first step is a private one. I put it first, because I think it is the most important of all, although it may or may not be first in time. It is to start making your own peace with God, by meeting with him by yourself in prayer. A second step, again not necessarily in sequence, is to become a member of a Christian church. A third step is to start considering in what ways, whether they be large or small, your manner of life may need to change. And a fourth step is to start advancing your 'education' in the Christian faith – particularly through reading the Bible.

In the rest of this chapter I will comment further on each of these four steps in turn, taking them in the order in which I have just mentioned them. But as I have indicated, the actual sequence in which you may take them can vary. Thus some people may choose to take the fourth step first, and go some way with readings of the Bible, before embarking on any of the other steps. Others may wish to start by attending some church services, and let each of the remaining steps follow later. Others again may want to take all four steps, in whatever precise sequence, with barely any intervals between them.

Of course, many would say that if you are going to become a practising Christian, then the quicker the better. That may indeed be so. But it has always been true that, while there are some who reach a point at which they are moved to 'plunge fully in', there are others who do not feel altogether ready for that, but are prepared to begin by walking a certain way into the water. And that is certainly better than remaining on the water's edge!

Meeting God in prayer

A vital step you will need to take, as soon as you feel ready to do so, is to start to bring yourself into a real relationship with God himself. This means meeting with him on your own, in private prayer.

Just what form your prayers should take on the first occasion must be between yourself and God. There are no rules to follow here. Only you can decide what you should say to him. It should be whatever you feel moved to say to him, from the depths of your heart.

So when you feel that the right time has come, go to your room or to some other place where you are unlikely to be disturbed, and open your heart to God in whatever way you are moved to do.

Do not be discouraged, if you feel that your first prayers bring no response from God. If over the following days you persevere in all sincerity – repeating the substance of what you have previously prayed, and perhaps adding some new prayers – God will surely respond, at the time he chooses; and when he does, you will receive the assurance that he has done so.

As your prayers continue, they could start to evolve into a certain regular pattern, or at least partly so. Here again, however, there are no definite rules about what this pattern should be: different people will develop different patterns of prayer, and this pattern can change as time goes on.

The next chapter seeks to offer some preliminary guidance, for those who are beginners in the practice of prayer.

Some people can feel that they are prevented from approaching God in prayer by a strong sense of their own guilt, as a result of their past life and the wrongs they now see they have done. The final part of this chapter, under the heading 'For those who have a deep sense of personal guilt', may be of help to anyone who feels to be in this category.

Joining a church

A second step you will need to take is to join a Christian church, assuming you are not already attached to one. However, you may possibly not feel inclined to become a regular churchgoer at once, particularly if you have seldom or never been to church services before, or have not been for a long time. You could then start with some relatively occasional attendances. (If you should feel hesitant about making your first visit, Christmas or Easter could be a good time for this. On these occasions there will usually be a fair number of others there who do not go to church very often.)

What follows is mainly for those who either are not sure about which of two or more different churches to go to, or are not much attracted by the prospect of going to church services of any kind.

You may well have a choice between different churches in your locality. If there is nothing that immediately draws you to one rather than to another, then it will be reasonable to take time to discover where you are likely to feel most at home before you commit yourself. Most churches welcome 'occasional' visitors, whether or not they are committed Christians; so you need feel no compunction about going, without any special invitation, to a service in a church where you have never been before. (And if, exceptionally, you feel you are not really welcome, then you will know it is not the right church for you!)

In Britain (and in a good many other countries too) especially if you live in an urban area, there may be a number of different churches within reach. In alphabetical order, the principal Christian denominations with churches spread more or less throughout England are: the Baptist Church; the Church of England (which is my own church); the Methodist Church; the Religious Society of Friends (the Quakers); the Roman Catholic Church; and the United Reformed Church (formed in 1972 by the union of the Congregational Church of England and Wales with the Presbyterian Church of England). In some areas there are also a number of other more or less independent churches, which go under a variety of different names. In Scotland, and again in Wales, the choices are somewhat different.

In what ways do these denominational churches differ? They differ to some extent in their official doctrinal beliefs (though not really in their central beliefs); they differ in their organisational structures; most obviously, they differ in the forms and 'styles' of worship that they follow. It is difficult, however, to generalise about their different forms and styles of worship, because these can differ quite substantially from one church to another within the same denomination (for example within the Church of England). Besides this, individual churches often have two or more different kinds of service at different times on Sundays, or different forms of service from one Sunday to another; many also have some form of mid-week service. Roman Catholic churches often have services on Saturdays, in the late afternoon or early evening, as well as on Sundays. You will really need to find out what are the different possibilities within your own area, and then try some of them out, if you want to find out what appeals to you most.†

† Among the churches I have specifically mentioned, the Quakers stand rather apart from the others in a number of ways, and much of what I say in this and the following paragraphs does not apply to them. They do not have any formal creed, and many Quakers have 'radical liberal' views about both the Gospels and Jesus Christ. They do not have services of worship like other churches, but hold Meetings in which periods of silent meditation are normally the central feature.

You may possibly be among those who feel reluctant to go to any kind of church service. Perhaps from your own past experience, or from what you have heard, you are not attracted by what normally happens in them (whether it be singing hymns, communal prayers, listening to sermons, or whatever); or you doubt whether you will have anything in common with those who go; or anyway, there are other things you would rather do with your leisure time.

How important is it for Christians to go to church services? There are different views on this. Certainly, for a great many Christians going to a church service every week is an important part of their Christian life, and something would be missing if they did not go. There are others who feel that about once a fortnight, or once a month, is enough. There are others again who do not feel that church services are very important for them or helpful to them.

In my own view, you should try out a number of different churches and forms of service before being ready to conclude (if it should in the end be your conclusion) that there are no church services that are right for you. Apart from anything else, church services are generally the main occasions on which Christians meet with other Christians and have the opportunity to get to know one another. Those who never, or hardly ever, go to church services are apt to remain a bit isolated from others who share the same faith. For most of us the friendship of other Christians is an important part of being a Christian.

Of course for those who are committed Christians the primary purpose of going to church services is to worship God. Or, to put it in slightly different terms ('worship' has perhaps become a rather old-fashioned term, of uncertain meaning), we go to church services primarily to express our devotion to God and to Jesus Christ. Through church services, along with others who are there, we gradually learn to come closer to God and to Jesus Christ. Cumulatively, we also learn more about what our faith should mean and are helped to live our daily lives better.

When in due course you have decided which particular church you wish to join and worship in with reasonable regularity, you should do whatever you need to do to become a full member of it. You will then effectively have joined yourself not just to a local church community, but also to the whole worldwide Christian Church – that is, the company of all those who acknowledge Jesus Christ as Lord, and who are committed to the work of advancing the purposes of God.

Church practices for becoming a full member differ from one denomination to another. You will need to find out what is the practice in your chosen church. Whatever else, if you have not previously been baptised, this traditional rite of entry will need to be performed for you. In the Church of England and Roman Catholic Church 'confirmation' is also a normal requirement. Where necessary, the two rites may quite possibly be arranged to follow one another in a single service.

Depending on your church, for practices differ here too, you may need to be a full member before you can fully participate in Communion services. The Communion service – variously called Holy Communion, the Eucharist, the Mass or the Lord's Supper – is usually regarded as the most important regular service of worship or devotion in the Christian Church. It is a service which in its central acts – the eating of a small portion of bread and the taking of a sip of wine – was instituted by Jesus Christ himself, during his last supper with his disciples before his crucifixion. It is the one form of shared devotion that has been made obligatory for Christians by Jesus Christ himself. As Luke's Gospel records, and also Paul in his first letter to the Corinthians, Jesus himself said we are to 'do this in remembrance of me' *(Luke 22.19, NIV; see also 1 Corinthians 11.24, 25).*

Christians have different views about how often we should take Communion. There are many who like to do so frequently and prefer most if not all of the services they attend (whether it be weekly or less often) to be Communion services. There are others who feel that a service of such importance should be something of a special occasion, not devalued by frequent attendance.

There is more about the Communion service in an annexe to the next chapter.

Churches do not have fixed subscription rates for members; but whatever services you may go to, it is normal to make regular voluntary contributions in one form or another, according to how much you can reasonably afford, towards the running costs of your church.

Making changes in your life

A third step you will need to take on becoming a practising Christian is to consider what changes you should make in your own life or behaviour. Only you can really decide, in prayer with God and with the Bible as a guide, what these changes, large or small, should be. Some may be changes to be made at once; others may follow later.

Advancing your education in the Christian faith

A fourth step you will need to take is to start to advance your own education as a Christian. Normal church services, with their Bible readings and sermons, should certainly have a part to play in this. However, simply reading the Bible on your own, particularly the books of the New Testament, is undoubtedly the most essential element of Christian education. For the Bible is in effect the primary 'source book' on every important aspect of the Christian faith. It also provides by far the best guidance on what it should mean to be a practising Christian.

Chapter 20 offers some guidance for those who are approaching the Bible for the first time, or who have not looked at it very much in recent years.

There are various other ways in which you can help to increase your own knowledge and understanding of the Christian faith, and of what it means to be a Christian. Among these are reading books on different aspects of the Christian faith, listening to religious talks or discussions on the radio or television, and joining some local Christian discussion group or Bible study group. Which of these you choose to do is very much a matter of personal preference, but many Christians have found that joining a discussion or Bible study group can be well worthwhile. Discussion or study meetings have a twofold purpose: to help people come to a fuller understanding of Christian thinking and of the practice of Christian life; and to help people to get to know one another. Alpha courses, as they are known, which follow a set pattern and are now held and repeated in many different parishes throughout Britain (and in a good many other countries too), deserve a special mention here. There are others also, with or without a brand name, that can be equally helpful (though with all such courses their value can depend in part on how well they are led, as well as on their content).†

For those who have a deep sense of personal guilt
People can sometimes develop a deep and overpowering sense of guilt, when they come to realise what the true nature of their past life has been, and to recognise some of the wrongs they have done. This sense of guilt and remorse is capable of being overwhelming, a paralysing burden on the mind and spirit. It may even be such that the very idea of living as a Christian seems impossible. How can someone who has done the unforgivable things that I have done become a practising Christian? How could I kneel down in prayer before God?

It has always been part of the Christian message that however great people's past wrongs may have been, they can never be barred from becoming practising Christians and starting to lead a new life. Provided they are truly penitent, however bad their previous life, if they ask for God's forgiveness they will receive it. They will then find themselves enabled to start living a 'new' and Christian life – and a life in which it will become possible to start making some amendment for whatever wrongs they have done – in the sure knowledge that they have become accepted, and are not rejected, by God.

This has been proved to be true, over and over and over again, in the life of the Christian Church.

This being so, you can be assured that, whatever you have done, there should never be any barrier to your approaching God in prayer and asking for his forgiveness. If you are fully repentant – if you sincerely acknowledge to God the wrongs that you see you have done, and really do wish to start amending your life – his forgiveness will come to be given to you; and when it is given, you will realise that it has been.

It can nonetheless sometimes happen that people find it difficult to approach God on their own in prayer. Or occasionally, repeated prayers

---

† The Alpha course, which I have specifically mentioned, has some critics as well as many supporters. Its standpoint is in certain respects more 'conservative' than that of this book; but participants are under no pressure to agree with everything that is said. With little doubt the majority of those who go on the course are glad they did so. My advice would certainly be to try it; you will not be under any obligation to complete the sessions, if you should find it unhelpful yourself.

may bring no awareness of God's forgiveness. Anyone who meets with difficulties of this kind may need the help of an experienced Christian friend, or of a Christian minister, priest or pastor, and should not hesitate to ask for it.

Should you become a practising Christian?

Of course my own answer to this question is yes. But I cannot decide for you.

You may possibly be one of those who, sooner or later, are more or less swept off their feet into becoming fully committed Christians. It is as though the decision is made for you; and where this is so, the experience can be that of having been directly claimed by God himself. But there are many for whom it is not like this, and if you are one of these many, you will probably want to reflect on what becoming a practising Christian seems likely to entail, before you make your own decision to move forward in this direction. What will it cost to do so, you may ask yourself? And what will be the gains in return?

Both the costs, or apparent costs, and the gains as you experience them, will depend in part on from where you start. The further away from being a true Christian that you start, the greater the costs of change may appear to be. But the greater also the immediate gains you will experience, once the change has been made. In what follows, I will assume your starting point is a fair distance away.

The main immediate cost, or apparent cost, is that you have to be prepared for change. You have to be ready to leave behind some part of your old life, and old self, in order to embrace what will to some extent be a new and different life, and to start to become, in some degree, a different person. Once you have committed yourself to the change, however, as you will almost certainly discover, what appeared in advance to be the costs of doing so are far surpassed by the gains you will find you have made.

You should be aware of some longer-term costs that may come later. To live as a practising Christian can at times be quite demanding or difficult – although it is not possible to predict in what ways, and how much, it may be so, as each persons experience can be different here. (Anything in life that is really worth doing is likely to be demanding and difficult at times.) Difficulties apart, to live as a true Christian could at some time become personally dangerous. This has not been the normal experience of Christians living in Western world countries over the past century or more; but it has been, and is, very different in other parts of the world, especially where Christianity is a minority religion. There have been many periods, and many countries, where Christians have suffered persecution, and no-one can say what the future may bring. Whatever may be the difficulties or dangers of living as a Christian, however, it is also the common Christian experience that God somehow helps us to come through them.

Now for the more immediate gains. The main gains you are likely to experience from becoming a committed Christian can be summarised under three headings, although in reality they are all linked together. You will discover the birth of a real relationship with God; you will experience a strong sense of having found a 'new' and better life; and there will be the start of a change in your own nature for the better.

God becomes real in a way that he never was before. We become aware that he knows us personally, and that he accepts us, and loves us, in spite of all the wrongs we may have done in our past life. We know that he forgives us. We have the sense of being in a 'right' and true relationship with him; we realise that we are one of his children.

With this comes a sense of new being, and of being 'alive' in ways that previously we were not; a sense, maybe, of having moved from darkness into light, and a general uplift of mind and spirit. We have a new sense of direction and purpose in our life; a sense of having found at last the right and true way of life, as God intends it to be. We can also have a new sense of freedom – of freedom from some of the bondages of our past life; we are no longer enslaved to the things of the world in the way that we were before. We have a new peace of mind. We have too a sense of 'belonging': we know that we belong to the company of all those who acknowledge Jesus Christ as Lord.

Linked with all of this, our own character starts to change, and to change for the better. We develop a new mindset, a new sense of values, a new vision of what really matters, and what does not. We become less self-centred, and more aware of the needs and feelings of others, more sympathetic towards others, and more understanding of them. . . But as we also realise, we still fall far short of being all that ideally we should be. . .

To become a practising Christian means committing yourself to a way of life that is bound to be different in some respects from the life you have previously been living. Whatever your apprehensions about this may be, if you do chose to become a true follower of Jesus Christ, you are unlikely to have any subsequent regrets. For whatever your new life may bring, wherever it may in the end lead, you will know that you have chosen the best road – the road along which God himself wishes us to go.

Chapter 19

An Introduction to Prayer

THESE few pages aim to give some preliminary guidance to those who are 'beginners' in private prayer. They start with some general comments about prayer and praying. The following section briefly outlines some of the main subjects for prayer. After that, there are short discussions, first on what our prayers can actually achieve, and second, on certain difficulties that everyone who prays can expect to find sooner or later. At the end there are some short prayers you could use, or re-express in your own words.

An annexe to the chapter contains an introduction to the Communion service, which is largely a service of prayer, and at its heart involves what can be seen as a special form of prayer.

Just what is prayer?
Prayer is our means of getting into personal contact with God. It is thus the main means of our developing a real relationship with him. It involves directing our whole attention towards God. We lift up our mind and heart towards him in trust that he is present with us.

At its simplest, prayer is 'talking to God', and normally our prayers to him will be expressed in ordinary words, whether said silently or simply thought. We can address him, as Jesus has taught us to do, as 'Father', and this word indicates the kind of loving respect with which we should speak to him. (Of course we should not forget that he is also the Creator of the universe!)

It is customary to kneel when praying, for this seems the most natural position in which to approach God. But we can in fact pray in other positions – standing, sitting or lying down. Whatever our position, it will usually help our concentration if we close our eyes, or cover our face.

Prayer can take a number of different forms, and there can be many different subjects for it. There is thus no single 'right' way of praying.

Though there have been various suggested 'methods' of prayer that can be followed, in the end we each have to find our own way of praying. And as our Christian life develops, the way in which we pray will naturally tend to some extent to change.

While our prayers should normally be addressed to God, they can alternatively be addressed to Jesus Christ, and many Christians like to do this sometimes. By long tradition, Roman Catholics quite often also pray to Mary the mother of Jesus; but this is not a usual practice for other Christians.†

Some main subjects for prayer

Some of the main possible subjects for prayer are briefly described below. The subjects we choose to pray about can differ from one day to another, though there will usually be a number of regularly recurring themes.

Before we start our particular prayers, we should normally spend some moments composing ourselves, recollecting that we are in God's presence. We remember who we are, and whom we are about to address.

An expression of our worship and praise for God

Though it may not at first come naturally to us, it can be good to begin our prayers with some expression of our worship and praise for God. By doing so, we can help to arouse within ourselves, at the start of our prayers, feelings that in time may need no deliberate arousing.

At the end of these pages there is such a prayer that you could learn to use; or you may prefer to make a similar kind of prayer in your own words.

Confession, and a request for God's forgiveness

We need always to confess to God the wrongs we can see we have done, and our failures to do things as we should have done them. We can then

---

† The reasons for the differences in practice go back into Church history. Christian devotion to the Virgin Mary, as the mother of Jesus Christ – the Mother of God, as she also came to be known – developed from around the fifth century onwards. At the time of the Reformation in the sixteenth century, the new Protestant churches drew back from special devotions and prayers to Mary, particularly because these practices were seen to have no scriptural foundation. Since then Protestant churches have adhered to this view, whereas the Roman Catholic Church, and likewise the Eastern Orthodox Churches, have continued to uphold the older tradition.

ask for his forgiveness, and for his help in enabling us to overcome our own particular faults and weaknesses, which make us so prone to go on acting wrongly.

Thanksgiving
From time to time at least, we need to thank God for the good things that have come to us – for the things in which we can count ourselves to be fortunate.

Prayers for God's help and guidance
A central part of our prayers will normally be to ask for God's help and guidance in our own daily life – for example, in whatever tasks we have to perform, and in whatever decisions we have to make. In fact, whenever we are faced by troublesome problems or difficulties, these will be subjects for us to bring before God in our prayers.

Prayers for our loved ones and for others about whom we are especially concerned
It is natural that we will wish to pray regularly for God's blessing on those who are closest to us. And we may wish to make some more particular prayer for someone who is faced with special problems or difficulties, or who is ill.

Prayers about the problems of the world, and for people who are in particular difficulty or distress
We may feel moved to pray to God about the problems and afflictions of our world. We can pray both for those who are suffering as a result of them, and for those who are working to overcome them or to bring help where it is needed.

Wordless prayer
As I said a little earlier, we should normally preface our prayers with a few moments of stillness, simply recollecting that we are in God's presence. Sometimes, in course of time, we may be moved to extend this usually brief period of quiet recollection into a much longer period – just holding ourselves in God's presence, without making any verbal prayers, and keeping any thoughts from flowing through our minds. This essentially is

the form of prayer known as 'contemplation'. It is a prayer from our hearts, rather than from our minds – a prayer of quietly 'waiting upon God', resting in his presence and 'opening ourselves up' to him.

What can our prayers achieve?

Can our prayers really make a difference? Can they somehow bring about a change in the course of events? Can they cause God to act in ways he would not otherwise have done?

There can be no simple answers to these questions, and in truth we know nothing for certain about the ways in which our prayers can actually 'work'. But there are some things that can be said. Let us start by considering our prayers for God's help and guidance in our own lives; and we will then go on to prayers of petition and intercession – broadly that is, prayers that particular things will happen and prayers on behalf of other people.

Our prayers for God's help and guidance in our own lives are certainly not going to make all our problems and difficulties disappear, or to make it always clear beyond doubt what course we should follow. When we ask for God's guidance over some difficult decision, he does not normally respond by showing us the right answer in some unmistakable way – nor of course are we made immune from the possibility of making mistakes! Most often, we can simply find that after due thought, and maybe also discussion with others, the best course becomes reasonably clear to us. A good deal more rarely, there can be certain occasions – perhaps when we have to take some fairly major decision affecting the future direction of our life – when we may end up feeling strongly assured that we really have been led by God to follow a particular course.

It is the common experience that our prayers for God's help in enabling us to overcome particular problems or difficulties really can result in our managing to overcome them, or work through them, better than we might have expected. Just how it is so remains beyond our real knowledge. Part of the answer may simply be that, as often happens when we discuss our problems with some other person, the very act of talking about them to someone who is listening sympathetically helps us to see things more clearly, and to see more clearly what we need to do, than when we merely think about them on our own. But quite apart from this, many Christians would say that it is largely through our prayers that we are able to receive the 'guiding, strengthening and sustaining' help of the Holy Spirit.

Turning now to our prayers of petition and intercession, it hardly needs to be said that we should not expect God normally to respond to our prayers by literally performing miracles – by intervening directly in the normal workings of our natural world. The evidence is that he will very seldom do so. Nor, from experience, can we expect him to intervene directly in the course of human events: as far as we can tell, he will never compel people to act, or to refrain from acting, in particular ways. On the other hand, it may be that, in response to our prayers, on occasions he will somehow gently move some person to act in a certain way, perhaps by in some way bringing a thought into their mind. Something like this does at times seem to happen. But here again, from experience, we have no reason to expect that it will always, or even frequently, happen. Very often our prayers do not seem to be answered! Or if in the end they are answered, it is in a different way from what we may originally have hoped.

As regards our prayers for other people, though they may not be answered in the way we would like to see (for example, through a loved one being cured from a serious illness), they may nonetheless be a means, in some way we cannot really understand, of bringing spiritual help and sustenance to them.

Because we know nothing for certain about the ways in which God may respond to our prayers or about what may determine his response, to a considerable extent our prayers of petition and intercession have to be 'experimental'. Or, to put it another way, we pray both in faith and in hope – in faith that God hears us, and in hope that he will respond. But whether God will in some way respond to a particular prayer, or there is no apparent response from him, it is natural (and it cannot be wrong) that when we meet with him in prayer we should go on expressing our deepest concerns and aspirations to him.

Some common difficulties with prayer
Probably everyone who prays regularly finds that there are times when prayer becomes difficult. Sometimes this may be related to certain distracting events that are happening in our life, sometimes not

obviously so. It may just be that our prayers cease to flow naturally; we no longer have any taste for praying; there is nothing we really feel moved to pray about. We can come to feel that our prayers are achieving nothing, and we no longer seem to be coming close to God – if anything the reverse. So we begin to wonder whether continuing to pray is really worth the time and effort it requires: perhaps we should give it a rest for a bit.

But, though it may possibly be helpful to try some rather different approach to our prayers, it is important not to give them up. For once the habit of prayer has become broken for any length of time, it can feel quite hard to start again. And even if our prayers are appearing to bring no kind of response from God, it remains true that – whatever the immediate appearances – it is really only through our prayers that we can go on being brought closer to God. And likewise, it is largely through our prayers that we can become enabled, through the help of the Holy Spirit, to keep on following the way of Christian life.

It is normally best to develop a habit of regular daily prayer, usually either at the start or end of the day, or both, even if only for a few minutes. And if the pressures of our daily timetable should be such that, most days, we find it difficult to manage more than some brief minutes for prayer, then we should try periodically to set aside a longer period, when our prayers will not need to be hurried.

Our regular prayer time apart, we can make brief silent prayers to God at any time of the day as we go about our life: for example, at the start of a particular activity; or just before the start of a meeting; or at the start of a car journey; or if we are uncertain about what to do when a quick decision is needed. For some Christians, this kind of prayer can develop into a practice that continues intermittently through the course of the day.

A similar longstanding Christian practice is to offer thanks to God at the start of a meal, sometimes also at the end of it. 'Grace' is the word normally used to describe this kind of prayer. It may be said aloud by one person on behalf of everyone present; or where this is not done, we can make our own short silent prayer of thanks.

Some prayers you could use
On the following two pages are some prayers you could use, either as they stand, or as a basis for creating some prayers in your own words. The first of them is the best known of all Christian prayers, the Lord's Prayer, the prayer that was given by Jesus Christ himself, when teaching his disciples how to pray. *(See Matthew 6.9–13; Luke 11.2–4. The two versions are slightly different, Matthew's being longer than Luke's.)* As you will be able to see, the separate prayers and petitions it contains cover a number of the main possible subjects of prayer. It is commonly recognised today that Jesus could well have meant the whole prayer to be used as a general pattern on which to build our prayers.

The Lord's Prayer has traditionally been very widely used just as it stands (although there have been a number of slightly different English versions of it). Used in this way, particularly if it is recited fairly quickly in a familiar form, we can rather too easily lose sight of the meaning, or perhaps meanings, of some of its phrases. I think it can help to re-express these phrases to a certain extent; and this I have done on the next page, alongside the prayer in one of its customary forms.

An Introduction to Prayer

The Lord's Prayer

A conventional form of the prayer	*A modified version of it*
Our Father in heaven, hallowed be your name, your kingdom come, your will be done, on earth as in heaven. Give us today our daily bread.	Heavenly Father, may your holy name be honoured, may your kingdom come, may your will be done throughout our world, as it is in heaven. Grant that our real needs this day will be met.
Forgive us our sins,	Forgive us the wrongs that we have done,
as we forgive those who sin against us. Lead us not into temptation,	as we should forgive those who have wronged us. May we not fall to harmful temptations.
but deliver us from evil.	Grant that we may be protected from the evils of the world in which we live.
For the kingdom, the power, and the glory are yours, now and for ever. Amen.	We proclaim that yours alone are the kingdom, the power and the glory, now and for ever. Amen.

A note about 'Amen'

It is the normal practice to end prayers used in church services, and on other occasions where a number of people are present, with the Hebrew word 'Amen', which is said by everyone, whether or not they have joined in the words of the prayer. Amen means 'so be it', and by saying it we give our assent to the prayer that has just been made.

A prayer you could say at the start of your prayers
Heavenly Father, may I draw closer to you now.
May I learn to pray as you would have me pray.

An expression of our worship and praise for God
Heavenly Father,
how great is your goodness, and love, and power, and glory!
You have made all things from the beginning;
everything in heaven and on earth is yours.
All the wonders of the world we live in are of your making.
We ourselves are your creation; without you we could not be.
So may your name be known, and honoured, and revered
throughout all our world.

A prayer for God's forgiveness
Father,
Please forgive me the wrongs that I have done.
Forgive me the things I should have done, but have not done.
Forgive me the things I should have done better than I did.
Please forgive me especially . . .

A prayer for God's help in our lives as Christians
Help me, Father, to see when I am wrong,
and when I am in danger of going wrong.
Help me to know my faults and weaknesses;
and help me to overcome them.
Help me to become more nearly as you would have me be.
Help me to live more nearly in the way that your Son, our Lord
and Saviour, Jesus Christ has shown us.
Help me, through your Holy Spirit,
to do always what is your will,
to serve you as well as I can,
and to love you with all my heart.

ANNEXE TO CHAPTER 19

The Communion Service

THE Communion service can be seen as essentially a special service of prayer. Mostly, the prayers that are spoken in the course of the service are addressed to God – they bring us into 'communion' with him. But at the heart of the service, in a particular way we enter into communion with Jesus Christ.

In what follows there is first a short description of the main part of the service. After that I will say something about the different ways in which the significance of the service can be understood.

The Communion service has been given different names – Holy Communion, Eucharist, Mass, Lord's Supper. Whatever name is used, the full service can take a variety of forms: different denominational churches use their own forms of service, and individual churches may also have more than one form of service in use. But in all churches the core of the service follows much the same pattern. We are retold the particular events, as they are related in three of the Gospels and in Paul's First Epistle to the Corinthians *(Matthew 26.26–29; Mark 14.22-25; Luke 22.14-20; 1 Corinthians 11.23–25)*, that took place during Jesus' final supper on the evening before his betrayal and arrest, trial and crucifixion. Thus (the precise words that are used can vary):

> At supper with his disciples the same night that he was betrayed, the Lord Jesus took bread and gave thanks to God; he broke it and gave it to his disciples saying, 'This is my body which is given for you; do this in remembrance of me.' In the same way after supper he took the cup and gave thanks; then he gave it to them saying, 'Drink this, all of you: this is my blood of the new covenant, which is shed for you and for many, for the forgiveness of sins. Do this, as often as you drink it, in remembrance of me.'

Following this, in whatever way is the practice within each church, a small portion of bread is eaten by each member of the congregation, and a sip of wine is taken.

Leading up to this climactic part of the service, which normally comes towards the end, there will have been spoken prayers and readings from the Bible. There may also have been some hymns and a sermon. To conclude the service, there will be two or three more prayers and possibly a final hymn.

The significance of the Communion service

Although there have been some different understandings among Christians of what the Communion service signifies, and these differences can be reflected in the precise form and words of the service, there is nonetheless a great deal about which many, if not most, Christians are broadly agreed. I describe below four different, but complementary, understandings of the service, which are widely accepted, although other Christians might express their understandings in slightly different terms from mine, and under the second heading there remains a well-known divergence of view, on which I will comment.

A celebration in memorial of Jesus Christ

Virtually all Christians are agreed that, whatever else it may be, the Communion service is a service of memorial and thanksgiving – a celebration, as it is often described – for the life, death and resurrection of Jesus Christ. The central words of the service, and the actions we ourselves perform in it, recall the words that Jesus himself spoke and what his disciples then did, during his final meal with them. By the re-presenting of his words, and the re-enacting of his disciples' actions, we are powerfully reminded of him and of the final events of his life. We are reminded both of the last supper itself and of the events that immediately followed – his betrayal, arrest, trial and crucifixion. We can remember too the momentous event of his resurrection two days later. Each of these events can be brought back to us. But especially the service is an occasion when we focus our minds on the most loving of all the actions Jesus performed, foreshadowed in the words he spoke

('This is my body given for you. . . This is my blood shed for you.') – the giving of his life, sacrificed for us all in the agony of the cross.

The word 'Eucharist', often used to describe the service and especially the central part of it, comes from the Greek word meaning 'thanksgiving'. An important purpose of the service is indeed one of giving praise and thanksgiving, both to God and to Jesus Christ, for all that together they have given us and have done for us. So in conjunction with its memorial aspect, the service is a shared act of thanksgiving and celebration: a celebration of God's love for us, and of Jesus Christ's love for us, and of all that their love means for us today, and will mean for us too in the future beyond death, to which we can look forward.

An act of communion with Jesus Christ

As most Christians see it, the Eucharist is more than purely a service of memorial and thanksgiving, or a celebration for its own sake. As Jesus surely intended, when he gave the words 'Do this in memory of me', we do it not just in memory, but also because of what the actions we perform mean for us who perform them. By what we do, provided we do it in the right spirit, we ourselves are drawn closer to Jesus Christ – we are drawn into closer communion with him. And we draw into ourselves something of his life-giving spirit.

It is here, however, that there are different understandings – broadly between the Roman Catholic and Orthodox Churches on the one hand, and Protestant churches on the other – about the way in which this happens.

Roman Catholic and Orthodox Christians believe that, when the bread and wine used in the Eucharist are consecrated by the priest who leads the service, while they continue to have the outward appearance of bread and wine, they are inwardly and invisibly changed, by means of a miracle, into the actual body and blood of Jesus Christ. This belief, which is known in the Roman Catholic Church as transubstantiation (Orthodox Churches do not use this term), is one that can be traced back to the beginnings of the Church, and it remained generally accepted until the time of the Reformation. It then started to become widely questioned within Protestant churches.

The traditional belief can be seen as supported by a literal understanding of Jesus' words, 'This is my body. . . This is my blood. . . ', and also by certain other New Testament passages understood in a literal sense *(especially John 6.33–35, 51-58).* Tradition apart, the theological debate about the different understandings of the Communion service here has largely centred on whether it is right to interpret the passages literally, or in a symbolic sense.

In New Testament times, the words 'body' and 'blood' will have been understood as signifying in a certain sense the whole of a person. To receive either the 'body' or the 'blood' of Jesus Christ was to receive the whole of him. For Roman Catholic and Orthodox Christians, who continue to follow the earliest traditions of the Church, to eat the consecrated bread is to feed on Jesus Christ and to receive him into oneself, in a very literal sense. In this way, those who receive and eat the bread, which has become his body, are united more closely with him, and are nourished spiritually to live more fully their lives as Christians. It is equally so when the wine is sipped.†

For Protestant Christians like me, who feel unable to accept the Roman Catholic and Orthodox teaching about what happens to the bread and wine when they are consecrated, while our understanding on this point is different, the effects of what we do can be seen as essentially much the same. For although the bread and wine remain for us just bread and wine, they are strongly symbolic of Jesus Christ, and we can be aware of his spiritual presence with us. Through what we do, like Roman Catholic and Orthodox Christians we are fortified by his spirit.

Whatever our belief about the consecrated bread and wine, in taking them we enter into communion with Jesus Christ, and unite ourselves more closely with him. Our sense of union with him is strengthened; something of his spirit is, or can be, imparted to us. ('Can be', because just what we receive spiritually will depend on the spirit with which we ourselves receive. If we allow our hearts and minds to be far away from what we are doing, we will receive little or nothing!) So it is that for all Christians, whatever the church to which we belong, the Communion service is, or should be, a source of renewing our spiritual energies and

---

† Traditionally, in Roman Catholic celebrations of the Eucharist, members of the laity have received only the bread, not the wine. The bread alone sufficed, being itself fully the body of Christ. However, in recent years this practice has changed, and in Britain and a number of other countries both the bread and wine are now normally taken by the whole congregation.

inwardly sustaining us for our daily lives, through being drawn closer in spirit to Jesus Christ.

When we eat the bread or the body of Jesus Christ (whichever it is for us), we are feeding spiritually on him, and similarly with sipping the wine. Much as ordinary food sustains our physical bodies, the spiritual food we receive in Holy Communion helps to nourish our spiritual life.

Something Christians do together

Though our personal communion with Jesus Christ lies at the heart of the Communion service, the act or actions of communion are not just something we perform by ourselves: we normally do them together with others who are doing the same. In the collective actions of the service we are drawn closer not only to Jesus Christ but also to one another. In the words that are often used in the service: 'Though we are many, we are one body, because we all share in the one bread' *(see 1 Corinthians 10.17, from which the words are taken)*. We come together in order to make a joint celebration, with Jesus Christ as our unseen host. Though we are all different, and may come from many different backgrounds, and though possibly we may hardly know one another (or sometimes not at all), for that short time our differences disappear.

What we do together on these occasions can be seen also, in a sense, to foreshadow the final realisation of God's kingdom in the next world.

The Eucharist seen as a sacrifice

Traditionally, and still so in the Roman Catholic Church, though less so in Protestant churches, the Eucharist has been seen as in some sense involving a sacrifice. There have been different views about in just what sense this is so. Perhaps most obviously, it can be seen as so in the sense that it always involves a re-presentation of the words that Jesus spoke at the last supper, words in which he anticipated his sacrifice of himself on the cross. On our part, when we are thus reminded of his sacrifice of himself made for our benefit, as much as we can we associate ourselves with it, and offer ourselves anew to God, in his service.

To put it a little differently, in the Communion service not only do we remember with thanksgiving all that Jesus has done for us; not only do we draw spiritual nourishment from what we do; not only do we join in fellowship with those who are doing the same: we are also making an expression of our devotion, and likewise of our commitment in service, to God and to Jesus Christ.

I have described four ways in which the significance of the Communion service can be seen. There is more too that I might have said. However, when we actually participate in the Communion service, it is best not to try to pass too many different thoughts through our minds. For most of us, it is enough to know that, together with others, we are meeting to celebrate the life, death and resurrection of Jesus Christ, and to be brought closer to him in spirit. In doing so, we also demonstrate our devotion to him and to God. At the heart of the service, our minds can be focused on the actions Jesus performed during the last supper and the words he spoke, which are re-presented to us. Then, when we ourselves eat the bread or his body, and sip the wine or his blood, in whatever way we may view them, we can receive into ourselves something of his spirit, to sustain us in our daily lives.

Chapter 20

An Introduction to Reading the Bible

THIS chapter aims to give some guidance on reading the Bible, for those who are not already familiar with it. It includes some advice on choosing a Bible, and also on obtaining a Bible Commentary or Handbook, to use in conjunction with your Bible reading.

As I said in chapter 18, Bible reading is the most essential element in advancing our education as Christians. The Bible is the primary source book on every important aspect of the Christian faith, and it is also the best source of guidance on what it should mean to live as a Christian.

This particularly applies to the books of the New Testament. Thus, from the Gospels we can learn virtually everything that is known about the ministry and teaching of Jesus Christ. Moreover, through their portrayal of his words and actions, we can begin to understand something of his own personality: as we read them, he can become increasingly 'alive' to us. Then from the book of Acts we can learn about the most significant events in the history of the early Church, during the thirty years or so after the death and resurrection of Jesus. And from the Epistles, we can see among other things what were the primary foundations of subsequent thinking within the main fields of Christian belief and practice.

Apart from what we can learn intellectually, reading the books of the New Testament can help to advance our own 'spiritual growth'. For when we read them, and reflect on what we read, we can start to absorb into ourselves their thoughts and values – the thoughts and values of Jesus himself. In this way we can actually be helped to become better Christians.

As many would say, the heart of being a Christian is to open ourselves up to the continuing influence of Jesus Christ – to the influence of both his teaching and his personality. The best way we can do this is by reading, and rereading, the Gospels.

Turning to the Old Testament, for ordinary Christians – it can be different for serious students of theology – its importance may be considered rather less than that of the New Testament, but there is a great deal in it that makes it well worth reading. Essentially, the Old Testament gives us the extended historical background to the coming of Jesus Christ and the birth of Christianity. It does so both in terms of actual events (although, particularly as regards the earlier events, there are uncertainties as to how much is factual history), and more importantly in terms of the development of religious thinking and ideas, and of ethical standards. We can read its books for their interest as historical documents of foremost importance in the development of religious understanding and beliefs, central to which of course is our understanding of God himself. Thus we can see the Old Testament books as portraying the history of God's revelations of himself to the Jewish people.

Though not everything in it is of equal value, there is much of great value in the Old Testament that we do not find, or do not find to the same extent, in the New Testament. Thus it contains most of what the Bible has to say on the subjects of social justice and the requirements of a just society; it contains some notable works of philosophical thinking; there is much more prayer than in the New Testament; there is much fine poetry; and there is some brilliant and enthralling story-telling.

Jesus himself quite often referred to the books of the Old Testament, and so also do the New Testament authors. There is quite a lot in the New Testament that cannot really be understood without reference to the Old Testament. This partly reflects the fact that, for the earliest Christians, there were no other recognised scriptural writings.

Choosing a Bible

There are today a number of English language versions of the Bible that are widely available, ranging from the now classic Authorised Version of 1611 to several different modern translations. It is undoubtedly best to buy a modern translation to start with, because although the literary quality of the Authorised Version remains unsurpassed, the modern translations are a good deal more readily comprehensible. In the New Testament this applies particularly to the Epistles.

An Introduction to Reading the Bible

In Britain the two most widely read modern English versions are presently the Good News Bible and the New International Version, and I think it will be sensible to go for one or other of these. (Other good modern translations are the New Jerusalem Bible, which is the Bible particularly used by Roman Catholics, the New Revised Standard Version and the Revised English Bible.) The New International Version is generally considered to give a more accurate translation of the Greek and Hebrew texts than the Good News Bible, and it is also perhaps of slightly higher literary quality – especially I would say in the Psalms and a number of other Old Testament books. The Good News Bible quite often provides a rather freer translation, particularly in passages where the meaning of the original text is somewhat obscure. The advantage of this is that the more difficult passages tend to be a little easier to read and follow than in the New International Version. For this reason, on balance it would be my own first choice as the best Bible to start with.

Another advantage of the Good News Bible is that it contains short editorial introductions to each book, which can be quite helpful.

Whichever Bible you buy, it is a good idea to get an edition that is well cross-referenced. For example, in the Gospels references should indicate where similar accounts of incidents, or of Jesus' teaching, can be found in one or more of the other Gospels. And where Old Testament passages are quoted in the New Testament, the references should show where the passages can be found in the Old Testament.

Bible Commentaries and Handbooks

Besides a Bible, you could well find it helpful sooner or later to acquire a Bible Commentary or Handbook. These essentially are explanatory books about the Bible, and again there is a fairly wide range from which to choose. The scope and coverage of each can differ to a certain extent; but generally they will contain chapters or sections, first, about the Bible as a whole (for example on how it came to be formed); second, about different groups of books within it – for example the Gospels and the Epistles in the New Testament, and the prophetic books in the Old Testament; and third, about each individual book. On the individual books you will find views on such matters as the authorship and date of the book, the circumstances under which, and purpose or purposes for which, it appears to have been written; and also some analysis of, and comments on, its contents. The shorter volumes will not give any verse-by-verse commentary; the longer, bulkier and more costly ones do so in varying degrees.

(For full-scale verse-by-verse comment you would need to obtain commentaries devoted to individual books, of which there are a large number. But these are generally written for serious students of theology and the Bible.)

I should add that Bible Commentaries and Handbooks are usually written from particular standpoints, as regards the 'inspirational status' of the Bible, on which views can range from conservative to liberal. If like me you cannot accept the traditional conservative view that the whole Bible is inspired by God in such a way that its authors were incapable of error, you will naturally prefer a commentary that does not take this standpoint.

The best and most helpful compact commentary that I have personally found is *The Hodder Pocket Bible Commentary*, which was originally published in 1962 as *William Neil's One Volume Bible Commentary*. It does not contain any specific section about the Bible as a whole (such as I have given in chapter 3 of this book), but the individual books are considered in their broader context. The style of writing may possibly seem a little 'dated' to some, but it is very clearly written, and easily readable.

Where to start

When you first get down to reading the Bible seriously, there is always the question of where it is best to begin, and what order to follow thereafter. For reasons that should be clear from what I have written earlier, I would certainly suggest reading the whole of the New Testament before you embark on the Old Testament, and the Gospels are without doubt the natural books with which to start. You could simply read through the New Testament books in the order in which they appear, and similarly in due course with the Old Testament. A possible alternative for the New Testament, which I think has quite a lot to commend it, is to start by reading Luke's Gospel first, immediately followed by his second book, The Acts of the Apostles, before returning to the other Gospels. For a good many Christians, Luke's is the most attractive of all the

Gospels; and to follow it by reading Acts will give a complete picture of events from the conception of Jesus through to the actions of those who, in response to their callings, established the early Christian communities.

For the Old Testament, many people may prefer a selective approach, rather than reading straight through from beginning to end; but there can be different views about which books to select, and I would hesitate to offer any advice on this. If you do read from the beginning onwards – and most people will want to read Genesis first anyway – you will almost certainly wish to do a fair amount of skipping. This could start with the later chapters of Exodus, from 21 onwards, and could continue through most if not all of the next book, Leviticus, much of which is concerned with detailed regulations for sacrificial and ritual practices.

Whatever sequence you follow you will probably want to do some skipping anyway, not just in the Old but also in the New Testament (for example in passages containing genealogies, such as at the very start of Matthew's Gospel).

Looking beyond your first complete reading of the Bible, there are a good many Christians who like to spend at least a short time rereading some part of it each day – often in conjunction with their prayers. There are others who prefer more occasional longer readings. But whether you come to read the Bible daily, weekly or less frequently, it is best if possible to develop some kind of plan for doing so; for otherwise months or even years can go by with it hardly being reopened.

Some 'difficulties' you are likely to meet
Some advance warning about certain 'difficulties' you are almost bound to meet in reading the Bible may be helpful.

You will very quickly discover that the books of the Bible are unlike anything else you have ever read. And you will probably also find there is quite a lot in it that leaves you rather puzzled, and uncertain about what you should make of it. This certainly applies to the Gospels in the New Testament, with which, as I have suggested, you should start your reading.

The Gospels have a unique style of their own (or perhaps I should say styles, for John's Gospel is noticeably different in style from the other three). Incidents are commonly described with a great economy of language, without any comment or explanation, although more occasionally the accounts do contain a fair amount of surrounding detail. But this usual brevity apart, there is quite a lot you are likely to find perplexing.

Depending in part on your own attitude to the possibility of miracles, this could apply to the (usually very brief) descriptions of miracles and other out-of-the-ordinary events. And it will almost certainly apply to many of the recorded sayings of Jesus himself, the meaning of which will often not be immediately clear.

The best advice, I think, is to read the Gospels, and likewise in due course the other books of the Bible, for what you *can* understand, for the passages that immediately speak to you – and not to worry too much about what does not seem to make any immediate sense. When you are not sure what to make of something, keep an open mind and pass on. Some of the puzzles you will find start to become resolved in subsequent readings, or with the aid of a commentary. But other puzzles can still remain after quite a number of readings.

On occasions the puzzles may be due to our having an inaccurate version of what was originally written, or in the case of Jesus' sayings, of what he actually said. Or sometimes, as I think can apply with certain passages in the Epistles, the author may simply have failed to express himself clearly. But we should not too readily assume such an explanation! And in fact, as regards Jesus' teaching, it seems clear that he often deliberately chose to use some fairly enigmatic forms of speech. Mostly, he did not want to lay down new 'rules' for people to follow. Rather, he wanted to challenge some of the accepted 'wisdom' of his day, to get people to see things differently, and to spur them into thinking for themselves in new ways.

A rather different kind of warning needs to be given about some of the things you will find within the Old Testament.

There are certain parts of the Old Testament where we see the portrayal of ethical standards that by no means equate with those of the New Testament, and which not infrequently appear nothing less than barbarous to present-day readers. Some of the most notorious examples of this occur in the descriptions of events leading up to and during the progressive Israelite occupation of Palestine (which probably took place around the thirteenth and twelfth centuries BC) and in the subsequent wars against neighbouring tribes. These include a number of accounts of wholesale slaughters of the indigenous population, including women and children, which on occasions – and many readers are particularly troubled by this – are represented as being directly in accordance with God's command.

While we cannot be sure to what extent the events described as happening during this period are historical (many scholars today would reckon the books in question contain quite a lot that is of doubtful historicity), it could well be that at least some such massacres did occur, even if not on the scale described. We should not of course imagine that God really did in some way order them to be carried out: it was the common convention for actions in the early course of Israelite history to be so ascribed. What rather I think we do have to reckon with is that up to the time when the books in question took something like their present form (perhaps somewhere around 400 BC, although probably in large part derived from considerably earlier writings), killings of the kind described were generally regarded as justifiable. This was perhaps especially because intermingling with local tribes who had survived the original Israelite influx was subsequently seen to be the cause of serious religious and moral lapses among the Jewish people.

Ethical standards have of course advanced very considerably since the times of the Old Testament. For though there have been all too many comparable atrocities in the later twentieth century AD, at least their occurrence is nowadays widely condemned.

Descriptions of particular events apart, it would be fair to say that the character of God as seen by some of the Old Testament authors is quite often markedly different from his character as revealed to us by Jesus Christ. Generally speaking the language used of God in the Old Testament is more colourful and imaginative than in the New Testament, and words are quite often put into his mouth. However, there are also parts of the Old Testament where the portrayal of God's nature is closely in line with the New Testament view of it.

Similarly with the expression of religious thinking and ethical standards: though sometimes primitive, at their highest and best the standards of the Old Testament are indistinguishable from those of the New Testament. In fact, what Christians know as the 'two great commandments', singled out by Jesus himself, and central to his teaching, are both taken from the Old Testament. The first comes from the book of Deuteronomy:

> Love the Lord your God with all your heart, with all your soul, with all your mind, and with all your strength.

The second is from Leviticus:

> Love your neighbour as yourself.
> *(See Deuteronomy 6.5; Leviticus 19.18; Matthew 22.35–40; Mark 12.28–31; Luke 10.25–28)*

The 'ten commandments' are also in the Old Testament, in the book of Exodus (*Exodus 20.1–17*). And another short passage that could be said to sum up fairly well the whole of Christian moral teaching is in the book of the prophet Micah:

> He has showed you, O man, what is good. And what does the Lord require of you? To act justly and to love mercy and to walk humbly with your God. *(Micah 6.8, NIV)*

In your first reading of the Bible, you will perhaps inevitably be rather in the position of someone on a journey of exploration in an unfamiliar country. To some extent this will be true of subsequent readings also, for in much of the Bible there is more to be discovered than we are immediately able to absorb. But as time goes on, you are likely to find that the Bible increasingly becomes a treasured friend and companion. To read from it becomes an illuminating and uplifting experience, a source of inner refreshment. Indeed, even at a first reading you will almost certainly find passages of which this is true – and passages to which you will wish to return.

CHAPTER 21

Christian Belief about the Holy Spirit and his Place in Christian Life

I believe in the Holy Spirit. (Apostles' Creed)
We believe in the Holy Spirit, the Lord, the giver of life, who proceeds from the Father and the Son. With the Father and the Son he is worshipped and glorified. He has spoken through the Prophets. (Nicene Creed)

IN Christian belief, the Holy Spirit is a divine 'person', who is in some way distinct both from God himself and from the risen Jesus Christ, but who at the same time is totally united with them. So it is that we have our belief about the 'Trinity' of three divine persons – Father, Son and Holy Spirit – who are distinct from one another, but who are nonetheless united together as one God.

As with God, the Holy Spirit is commonly referred to as 'he', without any intended implication of male gender.

The origins of our belief in the Holy Spirit, like all the main Christian beliefs, can be found in the books of the New Testament. It is grounded in part in the recorded teaching of Jesus himself, in part in various passages in the Epistles, and in part in early Christian experience. The most important instance of the latter, the coming of the Holy Spirit on the day of Pentecost following Jesus' ascension, was described in chapter 7. With regard to the teaching of Jesus on the subject, this is to be found mainly in John's Gospel. Here, as we are told, on the evening before his arrest and crucifixion, he said to his disciples:

> 'I will ask the Father, and he will give you another Counsellor to be with you for ever . . . the Counsellor, the Holy Spirit, whom the Father will send in my name. . .' *(John 14.16, 26, NIV)*

Many Christians have had difficulty in understanding what is really meant by our belief in the Holy Spirit. In what way if any is the Holy Spirit to be distinguished from the spirit of God himself, or from the spirit of Jesus Christ? There are those who would say that no distinction can really be made; but the Christian Church has thought it right to make the distinction. The true answer to the question must lie beyond our knowledge. It is part of the mystery of God.

For myself, I tend simply to think of the Holy Spirit as being a 'distinct part' of God. I think God himself must certainly be a 'complex' God, possessing many different 'aspects' – for example having many different 'centres of consciousness' and 'centres of activity'. Unlike human beings, he must be able both to be aware of, and to do, very many different things at the same time!

(The Church's doctrine of the Trinity – that God exists in three distinct persons, Father, Son and Holy Spirit, who share the same divine essence – can be seen as expressing something of the complexity of God's person, although that interpretation goes beyond the conventional understanding of the doctrine. The doctrine in its conventional form was developed during the first three or four centuries of the Church's life. Its underlying basis was the Christian experience of three different manifestations of God – God the Father himself, the spiritual presence of the risen Jesus Christ, and the Holy Spirit as a manifestation that was experienced as distinct from both Father and Son. In later Christian theology, the doctrine has come to be seen as linked with the Christian conviction that God is a God of love. Before there was anything external to God, before our universe could come into being, there had to be, and there was, the creative love of God – a love that must have existed from eternity within the Godhead itself, between Father, Son and Holy Spirit.)

The Holy Spirit can be understood as the spirit of God active in our world in certain normally hidden ways, helping and sustaining those who seek to follow the way of Christian life. He is 'God alongside us', or as Christians can ultimately experience, 'God within us' – not at all in any overpowering way, but in ways that are somehow supporting, strengthening, enlightening and encouraging. The main 'work' of the

Holy Spirit seems to be that of enabling us to develop whatever gifts each of us may have, to use in the service of God.

At the beginning of our Christian lives, as many would say, it is essentially through the enlightenment of the Holy Spirit that we first become able to see the truths of the Christian faith, and to recognise Jesus Christ himself as the Son of God. And it is with the help of the Holy Spirit that we are led on to become practising Christians.

The Holy Spirit can 'work' at times in a variety of other ways. Sometimes, perhaps once in a lifetime, certain people appear to have personal 'experiences' of the presence of the Holy Spirit. The book of Acts records a number of such occasions in the days of the early Church. Traditionally also, the Holy Spirit has been seen as the inspirer both of the Old Testament prophets and of the Bible's different authors (though there are different views today about the nature and effects of this inspiration). And yet again, in Christian belief it was through the power of the Holy Spirit that the miraculous conception of Jesus himself took place.

I do not think that Christians should worry about whether they have personally 'received' or 'experienced' the Holy Spirit, or about what he is or is not doing in their lives. The main thing is to seek as best we can to live as Christians. The Holy Spirit will then surely be helping us, whether or not we are ever conscious of his doing so.

Appendix

The Apostles' and Nicene Creeds

The following versions of the creeds are from the Church of England's *Alternative Service Book, 1980*.

The Apostles' Creed

I believe in God, the Father almighty,
creator of heaven and earth.

I believe in Jesus Christ, his only Son, our Lord.
He was conceived by the power of the Holy Spirit
and born of the Virgin Mary.
He suffered under Pontius Pilate,
was crucified, died, and was buried.
He descended to the dead.
On the third day he rose again.
He ascended into heaven,
and is seated at the right hand of the Father.
He will come again to judge the living and the dead.

I believe in the Holy Spirit,
the holy catholic Church,
the communion of saints,
the forgiveness of sins,
the resurrection of the body,
and the life everlasting.

Appendix

The Nicene Creed

We believe in one God,
the Father, the almighty,
maker of heaven and earth,
of all that is,
seen and unseen.

We believe in one Lord, Jesus Christ,
the only Son of God,
eternally begotten of the Father,
God from God, Light from Light,
true God from true God,
begotten, not made,
of one Being with the Father.
Through him all things were made.
For us men and for our salvation
he came down from heaven;
by the power of the Holy Spirit
he became incarnate of the Virgin Mary, and was made man.
For our sake he was crucified under Pontius Pilate;
he suffered death and was buried.
On the third day he rose again
in accordance with the Scriptures;
he ascended into heaven
and is seated at the right hand of the Father.
He will come again in glory
to judge the living and the dead,
and his kingdom will have no end.

We believe in the Holy Spirit,
the Lord, the giver of life,
who proceeds from the Father and the Son.
With the Father and the Son he is worshipped and glorified.
He has spoken through the Prophets.

We believe in one holy catholic and apostolic Church.
We acknowledge one baptism for the forgiveness of sins.
We look for the resurrection of the dead,
and the life of the world to come.

INDEX

Notes.
This index contains the more important references to each subject only; passing references are generally excluded.

Subjects listed under each main heading (e.g. Bible) are listed in alphabetical order, except that any general explanation is placed first, under a subheading such as 'general description'.

Abraham 130
Acts of the Apostles (book), general description of 16
Adam and Eve 6, 80, 100
    seen as mythological figures 101-2
Alpha courses 140, 141 footnote
angels 34, 66
    appearances of 34-5
    revolt under Satan, belief in 80
    traditional belief re origins of 80
Apocrypha, general description of 17-18
apostles 16, 40
Apostles' Creed 4, 172
ascension of Jesus Christ 51-2
atheists 5, 8
    atheist explanation of pain and suffering 110
atonement 80-1, 82-3

baptism 140
belief, differences among Christians, discussion of 74-6
Bible
    general description of 13-14
    Acts of the Apostles (book), general description of 16
    Apocrypha, general description of 17-18
    Bible as main source for Christian education 141, 161
    Bible as 'word of God' 14
    choosing a Bible 162-3
    Epistles, general description of 16-17
    Gospels
        general description of 15-16
        see also under Gospels
    historical reliability of Bible, general discussion of 19-29
    how and when Bible was brought together 18
    inspiration of Bible's authors, different views on 19-20, 74-5
    New Testament
        general description of 15-17
        earliest surviving manuscripts of 19
        importance of for Christian education 161
        reliability of present-day texts 19
        sequence to follow when reading 164-5
        see also under Acts of Apostles, Gospels, Epistles, Revelation
    Old Testament
        general description of 14-15
        authorship generally 15
        dating of books (mostly uncertain) 15
        difficulties met in reading 166-7
        historicity of 14, 33, 130, 167
        importance of 162
        miracles in 33
        Old Testament morality 166-8
        Old Testament view of God 167
        sequence to follow when reading 164-5
    reading the Bible 141, 161-8
        difficulties met in 165-7
        where to start 164-5
    Revelation (book), general description of 17
Bible Commentaries and Handbooks 163-4

Canticles (Song of Songs/Solomon), book of 14
Christ *see* Jesus Christ
Christian
    definition of 135
    should you become a practising Christian? 143-5

Index

steps to becoming a practising Christian 135-43
    educating yourself as Christian 141-2
    joining a church 137-40
    making changes in your life 141
    meeting God in prayer 136-7
Christian way of life
    becoming a practising Christian 135-45
    growing in love for God and fellow humans 96
    New Testament as best source of guidance on 161
    opening ourselves to influence of Jesus Christ 161
    the two great commandments 168
Church, church
    church services 137-40
    financial contributions to 140
    foundation of Christian Church 44, 69
    joining a church 137-40
    main churches in England/Britain 138
commandments
    the ten 168
    the two great 168
Communion service 140, 155-60
    significance of 156-60
conditional immortality 91
confession (of sins, wrongdoing) 147-8
confirmation 140
conservative liberal view of Gospels and Acts 20, 21, 29
contemplative prayer 130, 148-9
conversion, experiences of 135, 143
conversion of St Paul 54-6
cosmic theology
    definition of 78
    traditional Christian cosmic beliefs 79-81
creationists 6
    creationist beliefs re origins of universe 6
creeds
    general description of 4
    Apostles' and Nicene Creeds 172-3
crucifixion of Jesus Christ 41-2

Daniel, book of 14, 15
death, traditional belief in origins of 80
devil (Satan) 80, 82
    devil's responsibility for pain and suffering? 110, 111-12
    differences in belief re existence of 111, 125-8

differences in belief among Christians, general discussion of 74-6
disciples (of Jesus) 40, 46

education in the Christian faith 141-2
    Alpha courses 141, 142 footnote
    Bible as most important source of 141, 161
Epistles, general description of 16-17
Esther, book of 14
Eucharist (Communion Service) 140, 155-60
Eusebius (historian) 23
evil, different views re origins of 111-12
    traditional belief re origins of 80
evolution 6-7, 81, 100, 101, 103, 114
    God's chosen method of creation 100, 101, 103
    possibility of divine intervention in course of 101

fall, the fall of man, belief in 79, 80
    seen as unhistorical 81-2, 100-1
forgiveness
    God's forgiveness of us 82-3, 142
    our forgiveness of others (Lord's Prayer) 153
freedom of will, and its importance 102-3
'fundamentalist' beliefs about the Bible 19

Genesis, book of 80, 81, 100, 125, 130, 165
God
    essential characteristics of God, in Christian belief 1-2
    physical universe as evidence of his existence 5-8
    reasons for belief in God 5-12
    revelations of himself 8-12, 130-1
    why does he hide his presence from us? 129
God's purpose and plan in creation 84-5, 98-100
    summary of Christian beliefs about 3-4
    coming of Jesus Christ in context of 104
    evolution God's chosen method of creation 100, 101, 103
    future of souls that have not reached heaven 105-6
    second coming of Jesus Christ in context of 104-5
    traditional beliefs about 80-1, 100

Gospels
- general description of 15-16
- authorship
  - John 24 and footnote
  - Luke 24
  - Mark 22
  - Matthew 23
- author's intentions 26-8
- dates of composition 16, 22
- difficulties met in reading Gospels 165-6
- different views on historical reliability of 19-20
  - conservative/fundamentalist view 19, 21
  - conservative liberal view 20, 21, 29
  - radical liberal view 20, 28
- historical reliability in conservative liberal view
  - Gospels generally 20, 21, 25-6, 28, 29
  - John's gospel 26, 27 footnote, 71
- John's Gospel different from others 16, 26
- sources used by authors 21-5
- synoptic Gospels 16

guilt, sense of 137, 142-3

heaven, beliefs about 81, 94, 96-7, 98-9
hell 80, 81, 94-7
- modern beliefs about 96-7
- traditional beliefs about 94-5
heresies about the nature of Jesus Christ 72-3
historical reliability of Gospels and Acts 20-9
- conservative view 19, 21
- conservative liberal view 20, 21, 29
- radical liberal view 20, 28
Holy Communion (Communion service) 140, 155-60
Holy Ghost *see* Holy Spirit
Holy Spirit
- summary of Christian beliefs about 3
- coming of 52-3
- Holy Spirit in Christian life 170-1
- Holy Spirit and the Trinity 169, 170
- meaning of belief in 170
- origins of belief in 169

incarnation *see* Jesus Christ
inspiration of Bible's authors, differences of view on 19-20, 74-5
intercession *see* prayer

Jesus Christ
- summary of Christian beliefs about 2-3, 71-2
- ascension of 51-2
- atonement through his death 80-1, 82-3
- baptism of, by John 40
- birth, virgin birth (virginal conception) of 62-7
  - events surrounding birth 66
  - probable origins of belief in 63-4
  - radical liberal views on belief 64-5
- certainty of his existence 38-9
- crucifixion and death of 41-2
- divinity of 68-74
  - conservative liberal views on 74
  - probable origins of belief in 71
  - radical liberal views on 73-4
- future return (second coming) of 58-61, 104-5
  - different understandings of belief 59
  - expectations of early Church 59-60
  - origins of belief 58-9, 60
  - place in God's purpose and plan 104-5
- heresies about 72-3
- his early life 39
- his ministry of teaching and healing 40
- his nature and personality 40-1
- his teaching (in general) 40, 95, 96, 166, 168
- his teaching about God's purpose and plan in creation 79
- incarnation of 71-2
- last supper of 140, 155
- miracles by him 33, 40
- pre-existence of 70-1
- resurrection of 43-50
  - conspiracy theory 45-6
  - differences in Gospel accounts 43, 49-50
  - hallucination theory 46-7
  - radical liberal views on 47-8
  - resurrection appearances 43, 49-50
- second coming of *see above* future return of
- significance of his life, in God's plan 104, 131
- titles of
  - Lord 70
  - Messiah 68-9
  - Son of God 69-70
  - Son of Man 69

Index

Jewish religion at the time of Jesus 41
Job, book of 14
John's Gospel
    authorship of 24 and footnote
    characteristics of 26
    date of 16
    historical reliability of 26,
        27 footnote, 71
    sources used by author not known
        24-5
    see also under Gospels
John the Baptist 39-40
joining a church 137-40
Jonah, book of 14
Joseph, stepfather of Jesus 39, 63
judgement 81, 82, 93-7
    nature of 94-6
    timing of 93
    traditional belief about 94
        criticisms of 94-5

life after death 86-92
    reasons for believing in 86-9
    related issues 89-92
Lord's Prayer 152, 153
Lord's Supper (Communion service) 140, 155-60
love, as central to Christian life 96
'Love the lord your God...' 168
'Love your neighbour as yourself.' 168
Luke, author of Gospel and Acts 24, 55
Luke's Gospel
    authorship 24
    date 22
    preface to 27
    sources used 22
    see also under Gospels

Mark (John Mark), author of Gospel 22
Mark's Gospel
    authorship 22
    date 16
    sources used 22
    see also under Gospels
Mary, mother of Jesus 39, 62, 63, 67
    prayers to 147 and footnote
Mass (Communion Service) 140, 155-60
Mathew's Gospel
    authorship 23
    date 22
    sources used 22
    see also under Gospels

Messiah 41
Messiah, as title of Jesus 68-9
millenarianism 93
miracles
    are miracles possible? 30-3
        different views on 28-9, 30-2, 75
    miracles in Old Testament 33
    miracles of Jesus 33, 40
    a modern miracle 56-7

New Testament
    general description of 15-17
    earliest surviving manuscripts of 19
    importance of for Christian education 161
    reliability of present-day texts 19
    sequence to follow when reading 164-5
    see also under Acts of Apostles, Gospels,
        Epistles, Revelation
Nicene Creed 4, 173
non-Christians
    can they achieve salvation? 105-6

Old Testament
    general description of 14-15
    authorship generally 15
    dating of books (mostly uncertain) 15
    difficulties met in reading 166-7
    historicity of 14, 33, 130, 167
    importance of 162
    miracles in 33
    Old Testament morality 166-8
    Old Testament view of God 167
    sequence to follow when reading 164-5
oral tradition 15, 22-3

pain and suffering 109-124
    alternative explanations of 109-12
    could God prevent them? 115-19
    devil's responsibility for? 110-12
    functions of 113-15
        in our development as human beings
            114-15
        in processes of evolution 114
        pain as nature's warning 113
    God's responsibility for 122
    God's sharing in 123
    immediate causes of 115
    injustice of most suffering 121
Papias (early Christian writer) 23
Paul, St, conversion of 54-6

Pentecost, day of, coming of Holy Spirit on 52-3
persecution
   of early Christians 17, 54
   of Christians today 144
Peter, St (Apostle) 22, 46
prayer 89, 130, 136-7, 146-54
   nature of 146
   Amen, meaning of 153
   contemplative prayer 130, 148-9
   difficulties in praying 150-1
   Lord's Prayer 152, 153
   prayers to Virgin Mary 147 and footnote
   prayers you could use 154
   subjects for prayer 147-8
   what prayer can achieve 149-50
prophets 14, 33, 131
Protestant churches 15 footnote
Psalms, book of 14
Pseudepigrapha 79
purgatory 81, 94, 96, 97, 105

Q (as Gospel source) 22, 23
Quakers (Religious Society of Friends) 138 and footnote

radical liberal views on
   ascension of Jesus Christ 52
   divinity of Jesus Christ 73-4
   historical reliability of Gospels and Acts 20, 28-9
   miracles 28-9, 30-1, 32, 35
   resurrection of Jesus Christ 47-8
   second coming of Jesus Christ 59
   virgin birth of Jesus Christ 64-5
reincarnation 92
repentance 82-3, 142
resurrection of Jesus Christ 43-50
   conspiracy theory 45-6
   differences in Gospel accounts 43, 49-50
   hallucination theory 46-7
   radical liberal views on 47-8
   resurrection appearances 43, 49-50
revelation *see under* God
Revelation (book), general description of 17
Ruth, book of 14

Sadducees 87

salvation
   can non-Christians achieve salvation? 105-6
Satan *see* devil
scriptures 13, 17, 75
   see also under Bible
second coming of Jesus Christ 58-61, 104-5
   different understandings of belief 59
   expectations of early Church 59-60
   origins of belief 58-9, 60
   place in God's purpose and plan 104-5
Septuagint 17
sin, sins, sinfulness (wrongdoing, etc) 80, 82-3
   confession of 147, 154
   God's forgiveness of 82-3, 142, 147-8
   guilt for, sense of 137, 142
   repentance of 82-3, 142
Son of God (title of Jesus Christ) 69-70
Son of Man (title Jesus Christ) 69
Song of Songs, Song of Solomon (Canticles), book of 14
soul, souls
   nature of 89-90
   do all humans have souls that will survive death? 90-1
   first surviving souls in course of evolution 91-2
   souls of infants 91
speaking in tongues 53
spiritual experiences 12, 53, 56, 171
   see also conversion, experiences of
   see also God, revelations of himself
Stephen, St, martyrdom of 53
suffering *see* pain and suffering
synoptic Gospels 16

Taylor, James Hudson 9-10
Trinity, the, Christian belief in 169, 170

Unitarians, Unitarian Church 74

virgin birth (virginal conception) of Jesus Christ 62-7
   events surrounding birth 66
   probable origins of belief in 63-4
   radical liberal views on belief in 64-5

Wesley, John 10